Teacher's Book 5

Sandra Slater

Titles in the **Rainbow 2000** Series

	ISBN
Preliminary Pupil's Book	0-333-56857-5
Preliminary Teacher's Book	0-333-57020-0
Preliminary Flashcards	0-333-57090-1
Cassette Preliminary Book	0-333-57033-2
Beginning Handwriting Skills Workbook	0-333-57035-9

Pupil's Book 1	0-333-65140-5	Pupil's Book 3	0-333-65142-1	Pupil's Book 5	0-333-65144-8
Teacher's Book 1	0-333-65152-9	Teacher's Book 3	0-333-65154-5	Teacher's Book 5	0-333-65156-1
Workbook 1	0-333-65146-4	Workbook 3	0-333-65148-0	Workbook 5	0-333-65150-2
Cassette 1	0-333-65158-8	Cassette 3	0-333-65160-X	Cassette 5	0-333-65162-6
Pupil's Book 2	0-333-65141-3	Pupil's Book 4	0-333-65143-X	Pupil's Book 6	0-333-65145-6
Teacher's Book 2	0-333-65153-7	Teacher's Book 4	0-333-65155-3	Teacher's Book 6	0-333-65157-X
Workbook 2	0-333-65147-2	Workbook 4	0-333-65149-9	Workbook 6	0-333-65151-0
Cassette 2	0-333-65159-6	Cassette 4	0-333-65161-8	Cassette 6	0-333-65163-4
Flashcards Levels 1 & 2	0-333-65164-2	Flashcards Levels 3 & 4	0-333-65168-5		

Readers for each level are also available.

© Copyright Macmillan Publishers Ltd 1989
© Copyright adaptations for this edition Macmillan Education Ltd 1995

All rights reserved. No reproduction, copy or transmission of
this publication may be made without written permission.

No paragraph of this publication may be reproduced, copied or
transmitted save with written permission or in accordance with
the provisions of the Copyright, Designs and Patents Act 1988,
or under the terms of any licence, permitting limited copying
issued by the Copyright Licensing Agency, 90 Tottenham Court Road,
London W1P 9HE.

Any person who does any unauthorised act in relation to
this publication may be liable to criminal prosecution and
civil claims for damages.

First published 1989
British English Edition first published 1991
This edition first published 1995

Published by *Macmillan Education Ltd*
London and Basingstoke

Printed in Malaysia

ISBN 0 – 333 – 65156 – 1

Cover by Terry Burton

CONTENTS

Unit	Lesson	PB pages	WB pages	TB pages	Focus and Language
1	1	2-3	2	1	Revision *have to*; requests
	2	–	3-4	2	Revision *somebody* etc; numbers
	3	4	5	2	Revision comparison of adjectives
	4	5	6-7	4	Revision gerunds
	5	–	8-9	4	Revision numbers; dates
2	1	6-7	10	6	Revision Present Continuous
	2	6-7	11-12	6	Revision Present Continuous
	3	8	13	7	Present Continuous vs. Simple
	4	9	14	8	Revision Phrasal Verbs
	5	–	15-17	9	
3	1	10-11	18	11	Expressing future intent
	2	–	19-21	12	
	3	12	22	12	
	4	13	23	13	
	5	–	24-25	14	
4	1	14-15	26	15	*could* and *might*
	2	14	27-28	16	Consolidation
	3	16	29	16	clothing, holiday vocabulary
	4	17	30-31	17	Phrasal verbs
	5	–	32-33	18	Form filling
				20	TEST 1 (Units 1-4)
5	1	18-19	34	23	Revision of Units 1-4
	2	20	35-36	23	
	3	–	37-38	24	
	4	21	39	25	
	5	–	40-41	26	TEST
6	1	22-23	42	27	Revision clothes
	2	–	43-44	28	Revision
	3	24	45-46	29	Reported speech
	4	25	47	30	
	5	–	48-49	30	Listening comprehension
7	1	26-27	50	32	*so/because* in clauses
	2	–	51-52	33	
	3	28	53-54	33	Revision weather vocabulary
	4	–	55-56	34	Speaking exercise
	5	29	57	35	Family relations vocabulary
8	1	30-31	58	36	Comparatives and superlatives
	2	–	59-60	37	
	3	32	61	37	Comparatives in advertisements
	4	33	62	38	Degrees of comparison
	5	–	63-65	39	Vocabulary from context
				40	TEST 2 (Units 5-8)

iii

Unit	Lesson	PB pages	WB pages	TB pages	Focus and Language
9	1	—	66-68	43	Revision Present Perfect
	2	34-35	69	44	
	3	36	70	44	Present Perfect vs. Past Simple
	4	37	71	45	*for, since* and *ago*
	5	36	72-73	46	Invitations
10	1	38-39	74-75	47	Revision of Units 1-9
	2	40		47	
	3	—	76-77	48	
	4	41	78	49	
	5	—	79	49	
11	1	42-43	80	51	*want* + infinitive
	2	44	81	51	*like* + infinitive
	3	45	82-83	52	*prefer* + infinitive
	4	—	84-85	53	*try* + infinitive
	5	—	86-87	54	Listening for information
12	1	46-47	88	55	Infinitives of purpose
	2	48	89	55	
	3	49	90-91	56	Infinitives. Household words
	4	—	92-93	57	Infinitives. Town vocabulary
	5	—	94-95	58	New song
				59	TEST 3 (Units 9-12)
13	1	50-51	96	62	Revision question forms
	2	—	97-98	62	
	3	52	99	63	Revision question words
	4	53	100-101	64	
	5	—	102-103	64	Revision of numbers
14	1	54-55	104	66	Negative questions
	2	—	105-106	67	
	3	57	107	67	
	4	56	108	68	Reading comprehension
	5	—	109-110	69	Writing letters
15	1	58-59	112	70	Revision of Units 10-14
	2	—	113-114	70	
	3	60	115-116	71	
	4	61	117	72	
	5	—	118-119	73	
			120-121		TEST
16	1	62-63	120	73	Past Continuous
	2	—	121-123	75	Revision of time
	3	64	124	75	Past Continuous
	4	65	125	76	*while* in clauses
	5	—	126-127	76	Listening comprehension
				77	TEST 4 (Units 13-16)
17	1	66-67	128	80	Past Continuous vs. Past Simple
	2	—	129-130	81	Revision *when* clauses
	3	68-69	131	81	Occupations vocabulary
	4	—	132, 134	82	Revision time clauses
	5	—	133-135	83	Past Continuous

Unit	Lesson	PB pages	WB pages	TB pages	Focus and Language
18	1	70-71	136	84	Revision of adjectives
	2	–	137-138	84	Opposites
	3	72	139	85	Revision adjective order
	4	73	140-141	86	Verbs of the senses
	5	–	142-143	86	
19	1	74-75	144	88	Adjectives with *un-*
	2	–	145-146	88	
	3	76	147-148	89	Verbs with *un-*
	4	77	149	90	Parts of the body
	5	–	150-151	90	
20	1	78-79	152	92	Revision of Units 15-19
	2	–	153-154	92	
	3	80	155	93	
	4	81	156	93	
	5	–	157-159	94	TEST
				96	TEST 5 (Units 17-20)
21	1	82-83	160	99	Reported speech
	2	–	161-162	99	Tense shift present to past
	3	84	163	100	
	4	85	164-165	101	*if/whether*
	5	–	166-167	102	Listening comprehension
22	1	86-87	168	103	Reported questions
	2	88	169	103	
	3	–	170-171	104	
	4	89	172-173	105	
	5	–	174-175	105	
23	1	90-91	176	107	Revision of Units 1-5
	2	–	177-179	107	Revision of Units 6-10
	3	92	180	108	Revision of Units 11-15
	4	93	181	108	Revision of Units 16-20
	5	–	181-183	109	Revision of Units 21, 22
24	1	94-95	184-186	111	Revision
	2	94-95	184-186	111	
	3	96-97	187-189	112	Test A
	4	96-97	187-189	112	Test B
	5	–	190-191	113	Discussion of test
				114	TEST 6 (Units 21-24)
25	1-5	98-101	192-201	117	Revision of Book Five
TAPESCRIPTS				118	

INTRODUCTION

It is important that younger learners *enjoy* their first experience of a foreign language: one of the best ways of doing this is by adopting a teaching approach and learning materials which take account of the special nature of this age group, and which allow them to experience success by *doing* things in English.

The course
Rainbow 2000 provides young learners and their teachers with a large resource of material which can satisfy the demands of mixed ability classes and different rates of learning. There is a Workbook, a Teacher's Book and a set of tapes to accompany each Pupil's Book. There is also an optional set of picture flashcards for Levels Three and Four. Teachers are advised to make their own word flashcards, details of which are given in the Aids sections of the lessons.

The 25 units of each level are divided into five lessons. One lesson is intended to provide sufficient activities for a 45-minute period.

The background to Rainbow 2000
Rainbow 2000 has been written on the following assumptions:
- children learn quickly, but also forget quickly unless the items taught are frequently recycled.
- they need clear grammatical structures as a framework for language learning and use.
- children learn best through *doing*.
- written work can provide excellent consolidation for oral work.
- the subject matter should fit the age and ability of the child.

Teaching English with Rainbow 2000

Methodology
The Teacher's Book provides you with clear instructions on how to present the material to your children. This follows a pattern of LISTENING → SPEAKING → DOING, then SPEAKING → ASKING and ANSWERING QUESTIONS → READING and WRITING.

Language items are introduced with the help of demonstration, mime, real objects and flashcards. Children respond well to getting away from the pages of the course book, however motivating that may be, and every opportunity should be taken to reinforce the visual message of *Rainbow 2000* with objects from the children's real world.

Practice moves from *controlled whole class work* through *group and pairwork*, based always on carefully structured models, to freer *individual production work*. Language items are introduced, practised and recycled continuously, so that the children have the chance to practise again what they might have forgotten, and use the language items in new contexts.

The children are encouraged to move around and interact with each other. Some teachers may be worried by this; others will regard it as a normal part of teaching. Children have a great deal of energy and it is useful to let them burn some of it up: this leads to greater concentration in other, quieter, parts of the lesson.

In any case, there is no 'right' or 'wrong' way of teaching, and you are advised to adapt the activities to suit the needs of you and your own class: no two classes are the same!

Oral work

Pairwork   Detailed instructions for oral work between children and teacher are given in the lesson plans. The course also contains a lot of oral practice between pairs of children. This pairwork is very important because it gives *all* the children the chance to use the new vocabulary or structure in speech.

During the first week of term, show the children how to move quickly and quietly into their pairs. If they sit at double desks, there is no need for them to move. If they sit at single desks, they should move only themselves and their chairs. If there is one child left over, he or she can work with the teacher.

Most of the pairwork consists of either questions and answers or giving and obeying commands (*Point to the . . . . .*). They always follow similar practice between teacher and children so that the children have listened to and spoken the new language before they are asked to use it by themselves.

Using the tapes

Most of the new language is presented on tape. The general procedure is as follows: After the teacher has introduced the new language orally, the children look at the appropriate page in the Pupil's Book and get some idea of the content by looking at the pictures and words. They then listen to the tape twice, pointing to the words as they are spoken. The tape is played again, this time stopping after each sentence for the children to repeat. The teacher should help the children pronounce the words correctly and use the correct intonation.

The children then listen to the tape again and read along with it. Any variation in the usual method is given in the lesson plans. For example, sometimes the class divides into groups to read different parts or practises a conversation in their pairs. Sometimes the children listen for information, then respond to questions. When the children are familiar with the dialogue and understand it, encourage them to take parts and act it out at the front of the class.

Writing

In years five and six, the children are expected to write sentences and short paragraphs independently.

Workbooks

While the children are doing exercises in their Workbooks, always walk around the class checking their work and helping where necessary.

Use of first language

It is recommended that as little as possible of the first language should be used in English lessons although it is recognised that it may be sometimes necessary to do so. Try to encourage the children to work out meanings by mime or demonstration whenever possible.

Tests

There are five practice tests in the Workbook: a short test at the end of the Revision Units (Units 5, 10, 15 and 20) and a longer end-of-year test at the end of Revision Unit 24. The Teacher's Book also contains optional test material. These tests are located at the end of every fourth unit in the Teacher's Book.

Language Syllabus

The **Rainbow 2000** language syllabus is set out at the beginning of each Teacher's Book in the contents. It is not particularly extensive: since children need to have a lot of repetitive practice and recycling, it is better for them to cover a limited area of language more thoroughly.

Notes on the language forms used

Rainbow 2000 teaches the short forms *I'm, She's*, etc, from the beginning, without explaining their derivation. This is because it is more natural for the children to use these in oral work, and the long forms are introduced at a later stage.

Similarly, the form *I have* is taught, rather than *I've got*. However, teachers who feel strongly about this can obviously teach the alternative form.

Remember

- Read this Teacher's Book before you start the course.
- Always plan your lessons carefully; this Teacher's Book has been prepared to help you with your lesson-planning. It is easy to follow, practical and thorough. Your job will be easier and your lessons will be more effective and more fun if you let the Teacher's Book help you.
- Make lesson-planning an integral part of your teaching.
- Make full use of the Teacher's Book to ensure that both you and your pupils derive maximum benefit from **Rainbow 2000.**

UNIT ONE

Lesson One

Aim	Revision.
New language	None.
New words	*look after, busy, piano*
Aids	Tape 1a. A few different coloured sweets.

Listening and speaking

1 If you are new to the class, introduce yourself as follows. Say *Hello, children. I'm Miss/Mrs/Mr . . . .* Repeat several times, then prompt the class, then individuals, to say *Hello, Miss/Mrs/Mr . . . .* Prompt individual children to say *Hello, Miss . . . . . I'm . . . .* Walk along one row of desks and prompt all the children to introduce themselves in the same way.

2 Repeat with another row of children. This time after each child introduces herself say *Hello, ... How are you?* Prompt the child to respond *I'm fine, thanks. How are you?* and respond yourself *Fine, thanks.*

3 Show the children the sweets and ask a child *Would you like a sweet?* If the response is *Yes, please* ask *How about a red one? Would you like a red one?* Repeat with other children and other coloured sweets.

Listening, reading and speaking

1 Give out the new Pupil's Books and tell the children to look at **page 2.** Give them a few minutes to look at the pictures and read silently, then ask *How many girls can you see? What are their names? Where would they like to go?* Ask the children to guess the meaning of *look after* and *busy* and translate *piano*. Ask several children *Do you have to look after your little brother/sister? Do you have piano lessons?* Write some of their answers on the board for the class to read aloud eg *Mary has to look after her little sister. Jane has piano lessons. John has to look after his little brother on Friday morning.*

2 Write this question on the board for the children to read aloud. *Can the girls go to the cinema and see the new Stevie Spellbound film?* Tell them to listen carefully and then answer *Yes* or *No*. Play **TAPE 1a** once, and prompt the class to answer.

3 Play the tape again twice while the children listen, then divide them into two groups to read the two parts. They then sit in their pairs to practise reading the conversation aloud. They should use their own names.

Listening, speaking, reading and writing

1 Give out the new Workbooks and tell the children to look at page 2. Choose a child to read aloud the question at the top of the page, and then ask the class to use the pictures to find out why the children can't go to the beach. Complete the exercise orally before the children write the answers. Help with spellings if necessary.

2 **WB page 2.** The children sit in their pairs to practise the dialogues at the bottom of the page.

Lesson Two

Aim	Revision.
New language	None.
New word	*homework*
Aids	Tapes 1a, 1b.

Listening, reading and speaking
1 **PB pages 2 and 3.** Play **TAPE 1a** while the children listen and look at their books. They read the questions at the bottom of **page 3** silently. Choose children to read the questions aloud for you to answer. Then ask individual children to answer the questions.

2 **WB page 3.** Give the children time to look at the page silently, then ask them to explain what they have to do. Help them if necessary.

Speaking, reading and writing
1 The children sit in their pairs to discuss the order of the sentences. They should write numbers next to the sentences at this point. They can complete the speech bubbles later. Allow about ten minutes, then play **TAPE 1b** so they can correct their answers. The children then write the sentences in the speech bubbles and practise the dialogue in their pairs.

Listening and speaking
1 Use any time remaining to revise numbers and maths words in English, using any of the number games known to the children, either individually or as team games. Include *circle, square, round* in the game.

Lesson Three

Aim	Revision.
New language	None.
New words	*results, Grand Prix*
Aids	Tapes 1c, 1d.

Listening and speaking
1 Revise *somebody, nobody, anybody* as in Year Four.

Listening and speaking
1 *WB page 4.* Do the first three picture questions as a class exercise before the children circle the correct answers. They then do the word search and the drawings. Walk around helping and checking, and also prompting more children to introduce themselves to you. Allow them time to finish, then choose children to read aloud the twenty numbers they have found.

Reading and drawing
1 *WB page 4.* Ask the children to complete the boxes at the bottom of the page.

Listening and speaking
1 Revise comparative and superlative adjectives eg *big, bigger, biggest* and *difficult, more difficult, the most difficult* using classroom objects and children.

2 Ask the class questions like this. *Who is the tallest/shortest boy/girl in this class? Who has the longest hair/smallest feet? etc.* Let the children discuss the answers using . . . . . *is taller than* . . . . . */No,* . . . . *isn't as tall as* . . . . . */* . . . . . *is the tallest/has the longest hair etc.* Have the children stand together at the front so the class can compare them.

3 *PB page 4.* Introduce the new words using the picture.

Listening, speaking and reading
1 **PB page 4.** Play **TAPE 1c** while the children listen, then repeat with the children pointing to the correct driver as they listen. Ask the questions at the bottom of the page and prompt the class, then individuals, to answer. Choose individuals to ask the questions and you answer.

2 The children practise the questions and answers in their pairs.

Reading and writing
1 *WB page 5.* Read aloud the questions in the quiz, discussing at least the first few. Tell the children to ask for help with any words they do not understand. They then work in their pairs to circle the correct answers and then read their answers aloud. Walk around helping.

Listening
1 *WB page 5.* Practise this orally with some of the words from **TAPE 1d**, and prompt the children to say if they are the same or different.

2 Play **TAPE 1d** and have the children tick the correct answers in their Workbooks.

Lesson Four

Aim	Revision.
New language	None.
New words	*prefer, enjoy, reporter, love, hate*
Aids	Tape 1e.

Listening and speaking

1 1 Use **TAPE 1e** to introduce the revision. Play the tape twice while the children just listen with their books closed. Ask them questions eg *How many people are speaking? Are they men or women? What are their jobs? etc.* Encourage the children to guess the meaning of the new words from the context.

2 PB page 5. Play the tape again twice while the children follow in their books, then answer the true/false questions at the bottom of the page.

Reading, writing and speaking

1 *WB page 6.* Help the children draw the lines between the words and the correct pictures at the top of the page before they tick the correct columns at the bottom of the page. When they have finished, play the tape again so they can correct their answers. Now children make sentences from the table and their ticks, for example, *Saeed loves driving fast.*

2 Write these words on the board for the children to read aloud *like, don't like, love, hate.* Ask the children to put them in order.

3 The children complete ***WB page 7,*** then sit in their pairs to tell each other the things they like or hate doing.

Lesson Five

Aim	Revision.
New language	None.
New word	*diary*
Aids	Tape 1f.

Reading

1 *WB page 8.* The children can work together in pairs to link the numbers with the words. Then explain the way dates are written in numbers, and let them work through these together.

Listening and writing

1 *WB page 9.* Use the picture to teach *diary*. Explain the situation and what they have to do. Play **TAPE 1f** twice while the children listen. Repeat, this time stopping the tape to ask questions and to allow the children to ask you for help if there is anything they do not understand. Play the tape again while the children just listen, then give them another chance to ask questions.

2 Tell the children to be ready to write. Play the tape, stopping after Monday. Help the children to write the correct words in the diary. Repeat for Tuesday and Wednesday. This is a new kind of exercise for the children, and they may find it difficult. If they do, repeat for the other days of the week. If they are coping well, play the rest of the tape at once and let them complete the diary.

3 The children sit in their pairs to compare their answers, then play the tape again so they can check their answers.

Reading, speaking and writing

1 *WB page 9.* The children sit in their pairs to practise reading and spelling the words in the Word Box. Read out the words in a different order for the children to write in their notebooks. The children sit in their pairs, exchange notebooks and check each other's work using *WB page 9.*

UNIT TWO

Lesson One

Aim	Revision.
New language	None.
New word	None.
Aids	None.

Listening and speaking

1   PB pages 6 and 7. Give the children time to look at the picture, then say *Where are the children?* Prompt the children to make sentences about what is happening in the picture, using names or other means of identification eg *the girl skipping/sitting down etc.* Ask questions eg *Who's flying a kite? What is John doing? Is anybody sleeping/eating? How many girls/boys are sitting/jumping? etc.* Prompt the children to ask you similar questions.

2   PB page 7. Choose children to read aloud the sentences and say if they are true or false. Repeat, this time if the sentences are false, the child should say what is really happening eg *False. John isn't playing football with Walid. He's playing alone.*

Reading and writing

1   *WB page 10.* The children work in their pairs to write the answers then find them in the Word Square. While they are working, walk around asking individual children about the picture on **PB pages 6 and 7.**

2   Children who finish before the end of the lesson can write sentences about the picture in their notebooks. They should do this from memory, with their Pupil's Books closed.

Lesson Two

Aim	Revision.
New language	None.
New words	*mime, miming*
Aids	Tape 1a.

Listening, reading and speaking
1 PB pages 2 and 3. Play **TAPE 1a** while the children listen and point to the correct picture. The children then read the pages silently. While they are reading, write these questions on the board. *Who has to go for her piano lesson? Who has to look after her little brother? Who has to go to her grandmother's? Who has to go to her sister's?* Prompt the class to read aloud and then answer the questions.

Reading and writing
1 *WB page 11.* The children make eight true sentences from the lists at the top of the page. They can look at their Pupil's Books if they wish. Prompt the children to say two or three sentences orally, then either write the sentences in their notebooks or draw lines in their Workbooks. They sit in their pairs to check each other's answers, asking for your help if they cannot agree.

2 The children do a memory quiz. Emphasise that this is not a test, just a fun quiz to develop their powers of observation.

3 *WB page 11.* The children close their Pupil's Books and read aloud the questions in the Memory Quiz at the bottom of the page. They have three minutes to read the questions silently and try to remember them. Tell them not to write the answers at this point.

4 With Workbooks closed, the children now have five minutes to look at **PB pages 6 and 7** to try to find the answers and remember them.

5 With Pupil's Books closed, the children answer the questions at the bottom of *WB page 11.*

Listening, reading and miming
1 Teach *mime* and *miming* by demonstration. The children have encountered these words passively and should have no problems.

2 *WB page 12.* Choose pairs of children to read the two dialogues aloud, then the class sit in their pairs to mime and guess the words at the bottom of the page.

Lesson Three

Aim	Revision.
New language	None.
New words	*delivering, typing, postman*
Aids	Tape 2a. Pictures of people engaged in their profession – eg pilot in plane, a postman delivering letters, a typist typing etc. Pictures of famous singers, some actually singing, some not.

Listening and speaking
1 Use the pictures to revise and teach any new occupations and to introduce the new verbs. Use the patterns *What's his job? He's a postman. What does he*

7

do? He delivers letters. Extend the practice by miming occupations and asking *What's my job? What am I doing?* Call out children and whisper to them to mime one of the occupations for the class to guess.

2 Use the pictures of singers to revise the difference between the Present Simple and Present Continuous tenses. Say *This is . . . . . She's a singer. She sings. She's singing now. This is . . . . . He sings, too. He isn't singing now.* Repeat with other pictures.

Reading and writing

1 Write the new words on the board for the children to practise reading aloud.

2 *WB page 13.* Ask the children to read the instructions at the top of the page, then tell you in their own language what they have to do. They then work in their pairs to circle the correct sentences and write new sentences. Choose children to read aloud the sentences they have circled and written.

Listening and speaking

1 **PB page 8.** Give the children a few minutes to look at the pictures, then establish that the man with the tie is Peter. Ask the class to guess what the other man has been doing (painting).

2 Play **TAPE 2a** as far as *It's a great job* while the children just listen. Ask the children *What's Andrew's job?* and let them try to guess. Play the rest of the tape and ask again *What's Andrew's job?*

Reading and speaking

1 **PB page 8.** Play **TAPE 2a** again while the children listen and follow in their books. They then read the dialogue aloud in their pairs.

2 **PB page 8.** Ask children the questions at the bottom of the page. The children then practise asking and answering the questions in their pairs.

Lesson Four

Aim	Revision. Listening comprehension practice.
New language	None.
New words	None.
Aids	Tapes 2b, 2c. A radio or television, a large cardboard box.

Listening and speaking

1 Revise the following phrasal verbs by demonstration and mime – *take off/put on (shoes), turn on/off (a radio), get on/off (a desk), get in/out of (cardboard box).*

8

Give the children commands to do the actions, or to mime the actions for the class to guess. Let several children come to the front and give commands to individual children.

Listening, speaking and reading
1 PB page 9. Give the children time to look at the picture, then ask a child to read aloud the two sentences at the top of the page.

2 Play **TAPE 2b** twice while the children just listen, then repeat this time with the children pointing to the correct child in the picture. The children then read mother's words silently, asking for help with anything they cannot read or understand. The children then have five minutes to try to remember what mother said.

Reading and writing
1 *WB page 14.* The children complete the sentences at the top of the page, using the words in the box. Give them time to finish, then let them check and correct their answers by looking at **PB page 9.** Choose children to read their completed sentences aloud.

Listening, speaking and colouring
1 Spend a few minutes revising colours and numbers to ten.

2 *WB page 14.* Give the children time to look at the picture at the bottom of the page. Explain that these are clowns and tell the children that they are going to listen to a tape. The tape describes the clowns and gives each clown a number. The children must write the numbers on the correct clown's hat.

3 Play **TAPE 2c** twice while the children just listen, then twice again to give them time to write the numbers on the hats, and once more for them to check and correct their numbers.

4 Play the tape again five or six times while the children colour all the clowns according to the information on the tape.

Lesson Five

Aim	Revision.
New language	None.
New words	*frog, lay, tadpole, shrink*
Aids	A large drawing of a chair with a box and a pen on it and a cat and a ball under it. Coloured pencils for all the children.

Listening and drawing
1 The children need a piece of paper or their notebooks. Tell them to listen very carefully while you read. Say *Draw a big chair. Draw a box on the chair. Draw a pen next to the box. Draw a fat cat under the chair. Draw a ball next to the cat.*

9

Colour the picture. The chair is brown. The cat is brown and orange. The box is green. The ball is yellow, blue and red. The pen is green.

2 Tell the children that you are going to read this again, very slowly, and that you want them to draw what you say. Then repeat the description, reading each sentence two or three times, giving the children time to draw and colour according to the instructions. When they have finished, read the description again at normal speed. Let the children sit in their pairs to compare their drawings.

3 Ask the children questions about their drawings eg *What colour is the cat? Where is it? What's next to the pen? Where's the ball? What colour is it?* Let several children come to the front and show the class their drawings and describe them eg *There's a big chair. There's a green box on the chair. There's a blue pen next to the box etc.*

4 *WB pages 15 and 16.* Divide the class into pairs. Go around the class telling each pair who is A and who is B. Then say *A children, stand up. B children, open your Workbooks at page 15. A children, sit down. Open your Workbooks at page 16.* Tell the children that they must not look at the other child's page. One child in each pair describes the picture on their page for the other child to draw in the empty box on their page. When the first child has finished drawing, she describes the picture on her page for the other child to draw in the empty box on his page. When both drawings are completed, the children can check and correct their work using the other's pictures.

Reading, speaking and writing
1 *WB page 17.* Introduce the children to the new vocabulary, translating into their own language if necessary. Ask the children if they have seen frog's eggs and tadpoles and watched their development. Then give them a few minutes to read the passage.

2 Ask individual children to answer the questions. Then all the children can write the answers. This could be done as homework and checked at the start of the next lesson.

3 Practise the spellings in the Word Box on *WB page 16* to get ready for a spelling test next week.

10

UNIT THREE

Lesson One

Aim	To use the Present Continuous tense to express future intent.
New language	None.
New words	*boat, lunch, waxworks, Houses of Parliament, Tower of London*
Aids	Tape 3a. Pictures of London as above.

Speaking and listening

1 Check the children's answers to the homework question about the Reading Task on frogs.

Listening, reading and writing

1 *WB page 16.* Give the children five minutes to revise the spellings. Then read the words aloud in a different order for the children to write in their notebooks. The children then exchange books. Write the words on the board so they can check each other's work.

Listening and speaking

1 Use the pictures to introduce the names of the famous buildings in London, and introduce the idea of *waxworks*.

2 Play **TAPE 3a** while the children just listen. Ask them questions about what they heard, for example, *How many people spoke? Were they boys or girls? What were they talking about?*

3 **PB pages 10 and 11.** Play the tape again while they follow in their books. Ask them to guess the meaning of *lunch* from the context, and explain that *Evita* is the name of a play. Give them a chance to ask about anything they do not understand, then play the tape again.

4 The children practise reading the dialogue in their pairs. Choose children to read aloud the questions at the bottom of **PB page 11**, and other children to answer them.

Reading and writing

1 *WB page 18.* Give the children time to look at the notice at the top of the page, then complete the sentences at the bottom of the page orally as a class exercise before the children write in the words and then read aloud their completed sentences.

2 **PB page 11.** The children write the answers to the questions in their notebooks, finishing for homework if necessary.

11

Lesson Two

Aim	Consolidation of Lesson One.
New language	None.
New words	*pop concert, rock star, intelligence, stadium, concert hall*
Aids	Tape 3a. Pictures of rock star, rock concert, stadium. A poster, a notice.

Listening, speaking and reading

1 **PB pages 10 and 11.** Give the children time to read the pages silently, asking for help with anything they are not sure about. Play **TAPE 3a** while the children just listen.

2 The children read aloud the questions from **PB page 11** and the answers from their notebooks.

3 Use the pictures and the notices on **WB page 19** to teach the new vocabulary. Ask the children *Who's your favourite rock star? Have you ever been to a rock concert? Who was the rock star? Is there a sports stadium near here? etc.*

4 **WB page 19.** Go through the notices with the children, explaining *intelligence* by translation. Ask questions like this *Who's opening the supermarket/giving a piano concert/singing at the pop concert? etc.*

Reading, listening and writing

1 **WB page 20.** Do the first exercise orally as a class exercise before the children write the words to complete the sentences, and then read them aloud.

2 **WB page 21.** Let the children read the programme for the school trip. Talk about each activity briefly. The children can work alone or in pairs about the school trip.

Lesson Three

Aim	Consolidation.
New language	None.
New words	*play, theatre*
Aids	Tape 3b.

Listening and speaking

1 Talk about your plans for Friday, using known vocabulary and the pattern *I'm going to a film/a talk about dinosaurs. I'm watching a football game etc.* Ask children *What are you doing on Friday?*

2 **PB page 12.** Use the pictures to introduce and practise the new vocabulary. Encourage the children to talk about any theatres, plays or concerts they have seen, or any clubs they may know.

Listening, reading and speaking

1 Write the new words on the board for the children to practise reading aloud.

2 **PB page 12.** Play **TAPE 3b** while the children listen and point to the correct pictures, then listen and repeat the words. Ask questions like this *Where can you see a film/a football game/a play?*

Reading and writing

1 *WB page 22.* The children can use their Pupil's Books to help them with the first exercise. There are 25 triangles in the second exercise.

Lesson Four

Aim	Consolidation.
New language	*Good luck. Have a good time.*
New word	*luck*
Aids	Tape 3c.

Listening and speaking

1 Play **TAPE 3c** twice while the children just listen. Prompt the children to tell you what happened on the tape, who was speaking, what their names were, etc.

Listening, speaking and reading

1 **PB page 13.** Give the children time to look at the picture at the top of the page and to try to read the dialogue silently. Play **TAPE 3c** again while the children follow in their books.

2 Ask the children to guess the meaning of *Good luck* and *Have a good time*, and help them if necessary. Tell the children to read through the dialogue silently and ask for help with any words they cannot understand.

3 Play the tape again while the children follow in their books, then divide the class into two groups to read aloud the two parts.

Reading and writing

1 *WB page 23.* Give the children time to read the page silently, then choose children to read aloud the sentences at the top of the page. The children then work in their pairs to match the pictures and sentences and write the sentences in the speech bubbles. Walk around helping and checking their work.

2 When the Workbook exercise is completed, the children, still working in their pairs, read through Unit One in the Pupil's Book, asking each other and you for help with anything they are not sure about.

Lesson Five

Aim	To practise skimming for information.
New language	None.
New word	*orchestra*
Aids	Tape 3c.

Listening, reading and writing
1 **PB page 13.** Play **TAPE 3c** while the children listen and follow in their books.

2 Do the exercise at the bottom of **PB page 13** orally, then the children, working in their pairs, write two sentences each about Susie, Susie's cousin and Mr Short in their notebooks. Walk around helping and marking their books. As each pair finishes, they should practise reading the dialogue on **PB page 13** aloud. Collect in the notebooks for marking.

Reading and speaking
1 *WB page 24.* Give the children time to read the page silently, asking for help with anything they cannot read or understand. Ask the first three questions on *WB page 25* and help the children to find the answers. They have experience of skimming for information and should not find the exercise too difficult. There are a number of new words, but it is not necessary that the children should understand them all to find the information they want.

Reading and writing
1 *WB pages 24 and 25.* The children work in their pairs to find and write the answers, then read their questions and answers aloud. A few minutes before the end of the lesson, tell them that there will be a spelling test on the words in the Word Box next lesson.

UNIT FOUR

Lesson One

Aim	To use *could* and *might* to express future possibility.
New language	*I might go to the theatre.* *We could go to the sports stadium.* *I'm not sure.*
New words	*might, could, sure*
Aids	Tape 4a.

Listening, speaking and writing
1 **WB page 25.** Read the words in the Word Box in the children's own language and prompt the class to say the words in English. Give them a few minutes to practise the spellings in their pairs, then give them the test. The children can exchange books and use **WB page 25** to mark each other's tests.

Listening and speaking
1 Introduce the new language. Ask several children *What are you doing tonight?* Then prompt a child to ask you the same question. Say *I don't know. I might watch television. I might go to the cinema. I don't know.* Repeat this several times and then ask the class to guess the meaning of *might*. Help them if necessary. Teach the alternative form *could* in the same way.

Prompt another child to ask you the same question, and this time say *I don't know. I might watch television. I could go to the cinema. I'm not sure.* Repeat this several times, then ask the class to guess the meaning of *I'm not sure*. Help them if necessary. Ask other children the same question and prompt them to respond using the new language.

Listening, reading and speaking
1 Write these sentences on the board for the children to practise reading aloud: *I might watch television. I could go to the cinema. I'm not sure.*

2 **PB page 14.** Give the children a few minutes to read the conversation in the first picture, then play the first dialogue on **TAPE 4a** while the children follow in their books. Repeat for the other four dialogues, then play the whole tape while the children listen and follow in their books.

Reading and writing
1 Write this on the board for the children to read aloud and discuss.
> *I might go to town = I'm not sure.*
> *I could go to town = I'm not sure.*
> *I'm going to town = I'm sure.*

If necessary, get the children to explain in their own language.

15

2 *WB page 26.* Do the first four orally as a class exercise before the children complete the work, then read aloud the sentences and say if the speaker was sure or not sure.

Lesson Two

Aim	Consolidation.
New language	None.
New words	None.
Aids	Tapes 4a, 4b.

Listening, reading and speaking

1 PB pages 14 and 15. Give the children time to read the conversations silently, then play **TAPE 4a** while the children follow in their books. The children then practise reading all the dialogues in their pairs. You could ask five pairs to act out the five small dialogues at the front of the class.

2 Choose children to read aloud the questions at the bottom of **PB page 15.** The children then sit in their pairs to find the answers. Choose individuals to say the questions and their answers.

Speaking, reading, writing and listening

1 *WB page 27.* Ask children to read the sentences and look at the pictures. Then ask individuals to say what the six people are thinking. Ask them to answer the questions using *could* and *might*.

2 The children write their own answers and then listen to **TAPE 4b** to check their answers.

3 *WB page 27.* Working in pairs, the children sort the words into sentences. They then each write the sentences. Ask individual children to read their sentences aloud for checking.

Speaking

1 *WB page 28.* Use the language of the dialogue at the top of the page to talk about the first three photographs. Prompt the children to make suggestions using the same language. The children then sit in their pairs to decide what each thing is. Allow enough time for the whole class to discuss what each picture is at the end of the lesson. After the discussion, you can give the answers: 1 pens; 2 banana; 3 pineapple; 4 egg; 5 clock; 6 leaf; 7 jeans; 8 scissors; 9 onion; 10 lemon.

Lesson Three

Aim	Consolidation.
New language	None.
New words	*pack, swimming trunks, football boots*
Aids	Tape 4c.

Listening and speaking

1 Spend a few minutes talking about holidays and the different kinds of things you would take with you if you were going to a hot or a cold place. Teach *pack, packing* by mime.

2 Play **TAPE 4c** twice while the children listen. Ask the children to guess the meaning of *football boots* and *swimming trunks*. Play the tape again, this time telling the children to try to remember what Reda is taking on holiday. Let them tell you what they remember eg *He's taking an anorak and an umbrella.*

Listening, speaking and reading

1 **PB page 16.** Ask the children to tell you what they can see in the picture. Play the tape again with the children following in their books. Ask questions like this: *He's taking an umbrella/his swimming trunks/an anorak/his sunglasses/his football boots/three sweaters. Why?* to prompt the response *It might rain/be hot/be cold. He might swim/play football etc.*

2 The children read the dialogue silently, asking for help with anything they cannot read or understand.

3 Play the tape again while the children just listen, then practise reading the dialogue in their pairs.

Speaking and writing

1 **WB page 29.** The children sit in pairs to identify the objects, and say what Karim might do with them. Then they complete the sentences and you ask individuals to read their answers aloud.

Lesson Four

Aim	To learn some new phrasal verbs.
New language	*got up, give up, broke in/down, ran after/away, look after/for*
New word	*cigarette*
Aids	Tape 4d.

Listening, speaking and reading

1 Write these words in a list down the board for the children to read aloud: *give, sit, stand, run, break, look, shut.* Invite children to mime these words for the other children to guess.

Mime the words yourself, and tell the children not to guess until you ask them a question. After each mime is completed say *I sat down on a chair/gave Norman a pen/stood up/broke a glass/shut the window etc.*, then ask *What did I do?* to prompt the same responses.

Call seven children to the front and tell them to mime one of the words. The rest of the class must not speak. When they have all finished, ask the class *What did John do? Who sat on a chair? etc.* The class must answer using the Past Simple form.

Reading and writing

1 *WB page 30.* The children complete the page, then sit in their pairs to compare their answers. Choose children to read aloud their pairs of words.

Listening, speaking and reading

1 Teach the new phrasal verbs and *cigarette* by mime and demonstration, using both the *running after* and *ran after* forms.

2 Play **TAPE 4d** while the children just listen with their books closed.

3 **PB page 17.** Give the children time to look at the picture, then play the tape again. Go through the dialogue with the children, answering any questions they may have. Play the tape again with the children following in their books.

Reading and writing

1 *WB page 31.* Working in their pairs, the children complete the sentences without looking at their Pupil's Books. They can check them next lesson.

Lesson Five

Aim	Consolidation. Form filling.
New language	None.
New words	None.
Aids	Tape 4d. Cards with the bingo words from **WB page 32.**

Listening, speaking and reading

1 **PB page 17.** Play **TAPE 4d** while the children listen and follow in their books. The children then practise reading the conversation in their pairs.

2 *WB page 31.* The children check and correct their answers using the Pupil's Books. Choose children to read their completed sentences aloud.

Listening and speaking

1 **_WB page 32._** Give the children time to look at the page and then explain that they are going to play Bingo with words. They already know how to play Bingo with numbers. The children choose any nine words from the Bingo Box, and write them in the spaces in the Workbook.

2 Using the cards, read out the words one by one. If the children have that word written on their bingo card, they cross it out. The first child to cross out all his words is the winner.

3 Have the children copy the bingo card in their notebooks and write another nine words, then play the game again. This time, let one of the children read out the cards.

4 **_WB page 33._** Give the children time to look at the form, then go through it with them. They will need to know _international, male_ and _female_, but they may be able to guess the meaning of _penfriend_.

Reading and writing

1 The children complete the form.

2 The children should learn the words in the Word Box on **_WB page 32_** for a spelling test next lesson.

TEST 1 (Units 1 – 4)

1 Fill in the blanks. Use: | enjoy love hate prefer |

   1 I always play football. I _____ football.

   2 I often play football. I _____football.

   3 I play football and basketball. I _____ football.

   4 I never play football. I _____ football.

2 Circle the correct word or words.

   1 How many/much boys are fighting?

   2 Is somebody working/worked?

   3 They saw a play at the theatre/museum.

   4 What do you have/had to do today?

   5 Who is the eight/eighth girl in the race?

   6 How around/about this evening?

   7 'Wood/Would you like to go/going to the cinema which/with me
tomorrow night?'
'I'm sorry, but I can/can't. I had/have to do my homework.'

3 Quiz

   1 Which is longer? A metre or ninety-nine centimetres? _____

   2 Which is shorter? Two weeks or fifteen days? _____

   3 Which is bigger? A tennis ball or a football? _____

   4 Which is faster? A car or a bicycle? _____

4 Write three things you like doing. Use sentences.

   1 _____

   2 _____

   3 _____

5 Write three things you hate doing. Use sentences.

1 _____

2 _____

3 _____

6 Circle the four words that are wrong. Then write them correctly.

'Then after we had lunch we're traveling on boat on the River Nile and gone to Cairo.'

_____   _____   _____   _____

7 What am I?

1 I type letters. I'm a _____ .

2 I fly planes. I'm a _____ .

3 I deliver letters. I'm a _____ .

8 Fill in the blanks.

Morning School Trip To London

Saturday, January 12th

7.30	Bus leaves school
9.00	Stop for breakfast
10.30	Arrive London
10.30-11.30	Visit Science Museum
11.30-1.00	Visit Houses of Parliament
1.15	Lunch
2.00	Depart London
3.45	Arrive school

1 The bus is _____ school at 7.30.

2 They are _____ for breakfast at _____ .

3 They are _____ in London at _____ .

4 They are _____ the Science Museum and Houses of Parliament from _____ until _____ .

5 They are _____ lunch at _____ .

6 They are _____ London at 2.00.

7 They are _____ at _____ at 3.45.

21

9 Circle the correct word or words.

1 They might go/went to the cinema tomorrow.

2 My car broke in/down this morning.

3 The policewoman ran after/away the thief.

4 They should give away/up smoking.

5 I've lost my coat. I must look for/after it.

UNIT FIVE

Lesson One

Aim	Revision.
New language	None.
New words	None.
Aids	Tape 2b.

Listening, reading and writing

1 *WB page 33.* Give the children five minutes to read through their completed forms, then let two or three children read their forms aloud.

2 *WB page 32.* Give the children five minutes to practise the spellings in the box at the top of the page. Read out the words for the children to write in their notebooks. They can exchange books and mark each other's work using their Workbooks.

Listening, reading and speaking

1 Revise comparative and superlative adjectives using the children and classroom objects.

2 **PB pages 18 and 19.** Explain to the children what they have to do, then discuss two or three differences with the whole class. The children then sit in their pairs to find the rest of the differences. Walk around helping and joining in their discussions. Let pairs say one difference each until all fifteen have been named.

3 *WB page 34.* Give the children time to look at the pictures, then ask questions based on the incomplete sentences eg *Who is taller than Sarah/the shortest/the youngest? Whose hair is longer/shorter than Sarah's?* Let some of the children ask the class similar questions.

4 The children work in their pairs to complete, then read aloud their sentences.

Lesson Two

Aim	Revision.
New language	None.
New word	*guitar*
Aids	Tape 5a.

23

Listening, reading and speaking

1 Play **TAPE 5a** twice while the children just listen, without looking at their Pupil's Books. Ask a few questions eg *What's her name? Where does she live? How old is she? Does she like cooking? Has she any sisters/brothers?*

2 **PB page 20.** Play the tape again, this time with the children following in their Pupil's Books. They then read what she says silently, asking for help with anything they do not understand.

3 Choose a child to read aloud the questions at the bottom of the page and other children to answer them. They then practise asking and answering the questions in their pairs.

Reading and writing

1 **WB page 35.** Explain that the children are going to fill in the same form, but this time they must fill it in as if they were Sarah Martin. They work in their pairs and use **PB page 20** to help them. Before the end of the lesson, let children read aloud their answers.

Lesson Three

Aim	Revision.
New language	None.
New words	*hairdresser, names of countries*
Aids	Tapes 1a, 4d. Enough atlases for each pair of children.

Speaking, reading and writing

1 **PB page 5.** Give the children a few minutes to look at the page, then play **TAPE 1e** while the children listen and follow in their books. Ask the children to make sentences about the things Saeed loves, enjoys and hates.

2 **WB page 36.** Make sure the children understand what to do, then do the first sentence with them eg *I for insect, L for leg, O for onion etc.* Let somebody read the completed sentence aloud. The children work in their pairs to complete, then read aloud, the sentences and say if they are true or false. Finally, they make up a similar puzzle sentence themselves, and give it to their partner to work out and answer.

Listening and speaking

1 Give out the atlases to pairs of children and tell them to look at the page which has a map of the world with all the countries named. If your country is included on **WB page 37,** talk about that first, using the dialogue at the bottom of the page. If not, choose whichever is most likely to be recognised by your class. Help the children find the other countries on their world maps.

Listening and speaking

1 PB pages 2 and 3. Give the children a few minutes to read the pages silently, then play **TAPE 1a** while the children follow in their books.

2 *WB page 38*, Section One. Discuss the pictures with the children. Introduce *hairdresser* and write it on the board for the children to read aloud. Read aloud all the sentences on the left and prompt the children to point to the correct picture for each sentence. Read aloud the first sentence again, and prompt the class to complete the first sentence on the right. Repeat with the next two sentences. The children then sit in their pairs to complete, then read aloud, their pairs of sentences.

3 PB page 17. Revise phrasal verbs by playing **TAPE 4d** twice while the children listen.

4 WB page 38, Section Two. Let the children sit in their pairs and make as many sentences as they can. Walk around helping where necessary. Have a feedback session and write on the board correct sentences that the children read out. This activity could be set as homework and followed up at the start of the next lesson.

Lesson Four

Aim	Revision.
New language	None.
New words	*busiest, passenger, sound, fireman, engineer, air traffic control tower, baggage handler*
Aids	Tape 5b.

Listening, speaking and reading

1 Play **TAPE 5b** while the children just listen. Ask them to tell you briefly about what happened.

2 PB page 21. Use the picture and your own language if necessary to explain the meanings of the new words. Encourage the children who have been to an airport to talk about what they saw there. Ask them questions using the new vocabulary.

3 PB page 21. Play **TAPE 5b** again while the children listen, then listen and follow in their books, then listen and repeat.

Reading and writing

1 *WB page 39*. Discuss the trip to the hospital, using the language of **PB page 21.** Use the pictures at the bottom of the page to explain *porter* and *ambulance driver*. Let the children work in groups of four to discuss and write about the trip to the hospital. Walk around helping and correcting any mistakes. Choose children to read aloud their sentences.

25

Lesson Five

Aim	Test.
New language	None.
New word	None.
Aids	None.

Reading and writing

1   The children open at **WB page 40**. Explain that they are going to do a short test and that there should be talking. Go through the instructions for question one and make sure the children understand what they have to do. When they have completed question one, do the same for the rest of the Test, question by question. The children then read through and try to improve their work. Collect in the books for marking at the end of the lesson. The points are: 1: 5; 2: 5; 3: 5; 4: 10; 5: 18 (one for each word in correct order); 6: 7; Total 50 points.

UNIT SIX

Lesson One

Aim	Revision and extension of clothes vocabulary.
New language	*What size are you?*
New words	*striped, tight, cap, button, wellington, size, medium, light* (blue), *dark* (blue), *waist*
Aids	Tape 6a. Real objects to illustrate the words. Some very large and small clothes.

Reading and speaking
1 Go through the marked tests on **WB pages 40-41**, helping children to understand any mistakes they made, and practising anything which has caused difficulties.

Listening, speaking and writing
1 Get the children to try on some of the clothes to prompt the use of *It's too big/small/long/short*. Introduce *too tight* where appropriate. Teach the other new words by demonstration. Ask the children to come out and hold a button, a striped sock/scarf, a cap, a wellington, etc. Write the new words on the board for the children to read aloud. Call out children to sketch the meaning of each word next to it on the board. Leave this on the board for the children to refer to later in the lesson.

Listening, speaking and reading
1 **PB page 22.** Give the children five minutes to read silently. Explain *What size are you?* and *medium*. Say *My shoes are size . . . . .*, then ask several children *What size are you?* Play **TAPE 6a** in the usual way. Divide the class into two groups to read the two parts, then let the children practise reading the dialogue in their pairs. While they are practising, they should ask for help with anything they cannot read or understand.

2 **PB page 23.** Go through the questions at the bottom of the page orally.

Reading and writing
1 Working in their pairs, the children write the answers to the questions on **PB page 23** in their notebooks. When they have finished they should complete **WB page 42.** Walk around marking their work and helping where necessary.

27

Lesson Two

Aim	To learn more clothes vocabulary.
New language	None.
New words	*flowered, check, spotted, patterned, plain*
Aids	Tape 6a. Pieces of material as above. Aids from Lesson One. Coloured pencils for each child.

Listening and speaking

1 Use the aids from Lesson One to revise the new words.

2 PB pages 22 and 23. Play **TAPE 6a** while the children listen and follow in their books.

3 Use the pieces of material to teach and practise using the new words.

4 Give out the coloured pencils and use them to revise the colour words.

Reading and writing

1 Write all the new words from Lessons One and Two on the board for the children to practise reading aloud.

2 WB page 43. The children do the Memory Quiz without looking at their Pupil's Books, then work in their pairs to check and correct their answers using the Pupil's Books.

3 Working in pairs, the children write on **WB page 43** what their partner is wearing. For example: *She's wearing a blue striped T-shirt and a red skirt*. Choose children to read their sentences aloud to the class.

Listening and colouring

1 WB page 44. Give the children time to look at the picture. Ask them to point to the check/striped/plain shirt, the flowered dress/the patterned/spotted T-shirt. Tell them that they must listen to you, then colour the pictures. Explain that you will read through all the instructions first, then you will repeat them slowly, giving them plenty of time to colour. Read this aloud:

Colour the checked shirt black and red. Colour the striped shirt green and white. Colour the plain shirt grey. Colour one pair of jeans light blue. Colour one pair of jeans dark blue. Colour the spotted T-shirt with black spots. Colour the patterned T-shirt brown and yellow. Colour the plain T-shirt purple. Colour the plain dress blue. Colour the flowered dress green, yellow and orange.

Repeat the sentences slowly, giving the children time to colour. They then sit in their pairs to compare and check their answers. They should ask for help if they cannot agree.

Lesson Three

Aim	To learn reported speech.
New language	*She said the dress was too small.*
New words	*complain, behaviour, lazy, waste time, disturb, show off, boast, fight, pupil*
Aids	Tape 6b. Some of the big and small clothes from Lesson One.

Listening and speaking

1 Introduce the new language. This is quite a difficult new piece of language and should be introduced carefully. Begin very simply. Say *I like sweets.* Repeat this several times, then ask *What did I say?* Then answer *I said I liked sweets.* Slightly emphasise the *t* sound at the end of *liked* and repeat the answer several times. Write *I like sweets* and *I said I liked sweets* on the board for the children to read aloud. Draw their attention to the past and present forms of *like* and underline the two forms of the verb. Ask the question again and prompt the class to answer *You said you liked sweets.*

2 Call out six children and ask them each to say what they like to eat. After each child has spoken, ask the class *What did she say?* and help them to answer *She said she liked . . . . .* Call out another six children and give them the large and small clothes from Lesson One. They should try to put them on, then say *It's too big/small.* After each child has spoken, ask the class *What did he say?* to prompt the response *He said it was too big/small.*

Listening, reading and speaking

1 *WB page 45.* The children look at the picture at the top of the page and then read the monologue silently. Ask them to guess the meaning of *complain* and help them if necessary. Read the monologue aloud, then have the children read the sentences aloud around the class.

2 *WB page 45.* Look at the second picture. Establish that the woman is the shop assistant from the first picture, and that she is telling somebody what the customer in the first picture said. Read aloud the monologue from the second picture, then have the children read the sentences aloud around the class. Then underline the differences between the two sets of sentences as a class exercise.

Listening, reading and speaking

1 *PB page 24.* Play **TAPE 6b** while the children look at the picture. Go through the monologue prompting the children to guess the meanings of the new words and helping them where necessary. Play the tape again while the class follow in their books, then again while the class listen and repeat. Write all the new words on the board for the children to practise reading aloud. Point to each word in turn and ask the class to translate into their own language. The children then read the page silently, asking for help with anything they cannot read or understand.

29

Lesson Four

Aim	Consolidation of Lesson Three.
New language	None.
New words	*worried, traffic*
Aids	Tapes 6b, 6c, 6d.

Listening and speaking
1 Spend a few minutes revising reported speech as in Lesson Three.

2 PB page 24. Play **TAPE 6b** while the children listen and follow in their books.

Listening, reading and writing
1 *WB page 46.* Make sure the children understand that this is Alex, the boy from **PB page 24**. He is telling his friend what the school principal said to him. Complete the first five sentences as a class exercise, then the children complete the work in their pairs. Walk around helping and checking while they work. When they have finished, play **TAPE 6c** several times so they can check their work.

Writing
1 *WB page 47.* Explain to the children that they must complete the sentences, to show what the four people said. The children then complete the sentences, working in their pairs. Choose children to read aloud their completed sentences at the end of the lesson.

Listening, speaking, reading and writing
1 PB page 25. The children read the newspaper article. Ask them to find the two new words and prompt the children to guess their meaning. Ask if there are any other words they cannot read or understand. Write the new words and other words they have asked about on the board for the children to practise reading aloud. Working in their pairs, the children read the passage again silently, then ask and answer the questions at the bottom of the page. Choose pairs of children to read the questions and give their answers.

2 *WB page 47.* Go through the exercise orally before the children, working in their pairs, begin to write. When they have all finished, play **TAPE 6d** several times so they can check and correct what they have written.

Lesson Five

Aim	Listening comprehension.
New language	None.
New words	None.
Aids	Tape 6e.

30

Drawing and writing

1 *WB pages 42 and 43.* Use these pages to revise the names of clothes and types of patterns.

2 *WB page 48.* Give the children time to read the instructions aloud, and then ask them to explain in their own language what they have to do. Allow five to ten minutes for the colouring, then the children should write the descriptions. Walk around helping and checking. When they have finished, the children sit in their pairs, exchange books and check each other's work. If they cannot agree, they should ask for your help.

3 Set the final task on *WB page 49* for homework.

Listening and writing

1 The listening comprehension exercise is quite long and the children are not expected to be able to understand every single word. Make sure they are aware of this.

2 *WB page 49.* Give the children time to read the words in the boxes, and tell them that they have to listen to the tape and then tick the correct item in each box. Play the whole of **TAPE 6e** twice while the children just listen to familiarise themselves with what is going on. Play it again, section by section, so they can complete each section of the checklist. Repeat as many times as they need. Finally, play through the whole tape again for them to check their answers.

3 The children, working in their pairs, learn the spellings in the Word Box on *WB page 49,* ready for a spelling test next lesson.

UNIT SEVEN

Lesson One

Aim	To use clauses with *so* and *because*.
New language	*I didn't. . . ., so/because I. . . . .*
New words	*so, boring, waited, tourists*
Aids	Tape 7a.

Reading and writing
1 Do the spelling test in the usual way.

Listening, reading and speaking
1 Introduce the new language. Ask a child *Did you come to school yesterday?* to prompt the response *No, I didn't*. Write this on the board: *Anna didn't come to school yesterday* (no full stop). Ask her why, prompting her to answer *because. . . . .* Add her answer to the first sentence eg *Anna didn't come to school yesterday because it was Friday*. Ask other children the same question and if they have different answers, write them on the board.

2 Say *I didn't come to school on Friday, so I went swimming*. Repeat several times, then write the sentence on the board. Prompt the children to repeat the sentence, adding their own ending, eg *I didn't come to school on Friday, so I played football/listened to my records/went to my grandmother's etc*.

3 Play **TAPE 7a** twice while the children just listen. Ask them a few simple questions eg *How many people are talking? Are they boys or girls? What are they talking about?*

4 **PB pages 26 and 27.** Play the tape again while the children follow in their books. Teach the new words. Ask more difficult questions eg *Who went on holiday? Where did she go? Why didn't she go to Greece? Did she bring anything back? What was it?* The children then read through the conversation silently, asking for help with anything they do not understand.

5 The children practise reading the conversation in their pairs and ask and answer the questions at the bottom of **PB page 27**.

Reading and writing
1 ***WB page 50.*** The children work in their pairs to complete, then read aloud, the sentences. They should use the Pupil's Book to help them.

32

Lesson Two

Aim	Consolidation of Lesson One.
New language	None.
New words	None.
Aids	Tapes 7a, 7b.

Listening, reading and speaking
1   PB pages 26 and 27. Play **TAPE 7a** while the children listen and follow in their books.

2   Practise the difference between *so* and *because*. Write this on the board for the children to read aloud:
   John ate three ice creams because it was very hot.
   Mary ate three ice creams so she was sick.
Ask the children to suggest other endings, and write their sentences on the board.

3   Write these sentences on the board and ask the class to finish them using *so* or *because*.
   Sarah went to her grandfather's house because . . . . .
   Sarah went to her grandfather's house, so . . . . .

4   Play **TAPE 7b** twice while the children listen. Ask them to explain briefly in their own language what happened. They then look at the pictures on **WB page 51**, and read the sentences silently. Choose children to read the sentences aloud. Explain what they have to do, then play **TAPE 7b** again while the children listen. They then work in their pairs to put the sentences into the correct order. Play the tape again, so they can correct their work.

Reading, writing and drawing
1   WB page 52. The children complete the exercise. Walk around helping and checking their work.

Lesson Three

Aim	Consolidation. Revision of weather vocabulary.
New language	None.
New words	*picnic, ice skating, snowman, surfing, barbecue, really, avalanche, crash (v), crystals, dangerous, freeze, plough, sledge (v), snowball*
Aids	Tape 7c. Pictures of snow scenes.

33

Listening and speaking
1   Use the pictures on **PB page 28** to teach the new words.

Listening, speaking and reading
1   Write the new words on the board for the children to read aloud and spell.

2   **PB page 28.** Ask the children to find and read aloud the sentences containing the new words. Play **TAPE 7c** twice while the children follow in their books, then listen and repeat. Ask the questions at the bottom of the page and choose children to answer. The children then read the page silently, asking for help if necessary, and sit in their pairs to practise asking and answering the questions.

Reading and speaking
1   **WB page 53.** Introduce the children to the new vocabulary in the usual way. Many children will never have seen snow. Using pictures of snow scenes, help them to understand what it is like and to understand the words better.

2   The children read the page silently, asking for help if necessary, and then sit in pairs to choose the answers to the questions on **WB page 54**. Ask individuals to read out their answers.

Lesson Four

Aim	Speaking exercise.
New language	None.
New words	None.
Aids	Tape 7a.

Listening, speaking and reading
1   **PB pages 26 and 27.** Play **TAPE 7a** while the children listen and follow in their books. Choose children to read aloud the questions at the bottom of the page and other children to answer them. The children then practise the questions and answers in their pairs.

2   **WB pages 55 and 56.** Still in their pairs, the children do a speaking exercise. Walk around the class, telling each pair which is number one and which is number two. Tell the number one children to open their Workbooks at page 55. The number two children open their Workbooks at page 56. They must not look at each other's pages. The object of the exercise is to complete the table by asking each other questions. Each child has half the table on his page, so they must ask their partners questions in order to complete their tables. Demonstrate what to do. Ask *What was the weather like in London on Monday?* to prompt the response *Wet*. Then ask *What was the weather like in London on Tuesday?* to prompt the response *Wet*. The children should take turns to ask questions. When they have finished, ask individual children questions before they check their answers by looking at both pages together.

3   Finish the lesson with the crossword on **WB page 55.**

34

Lesson Five

Aim	Revision of family relationships.
New language	My brother is called Tom.
New word	called
Aids	Tape 7d.

Listening, reading and speaking
1 PB page 29. Give the children time to look at the family tree, and remind them that Ryan is the Australian boy they read about on **PB page 28.** Ask the children to find Ryan on the family tree. Ask the children to find Ryan's sister and say Ryan's sister is called Helen. Repeat this several times, then ask individuals Do you have a sister? What's she called? to prompt the response She's called . . . . .

2 Play **TAPE 7d** while the children listen and look at the family tree, then repeat while the children follow the text. The children then read the text silently, asking for help with anything they cannot understand.

3 Ask questions about Ryan's family, using the patterns What's Ryan's sister/mother called? What are Ryan's brothers/uncles/grandmothers/aunts called? Prompt the class to ask you similar questions.

Listening, reading and speaking
1 WB page 57. The children complete the family tree, working in their pairs. They can find the information in the Pupil's Book or by listening to **TAPE 7d**, which you should play several times while they are working. When they have finished, they sit in their pairs to compare and check their answers.

Writing
1 PB page 29. The children write the completed sentences from the bottom of the page in their notebooks. Choose children to read aloud their completed sentences.

2 The children learn the spelling of the words in the Word Box on **WB page 57** ready for a test next lesson.

35

UNIT EIGHT

Lesson One

Aim	Revision of comparatives and superlatives.
New language	None.
New word	*complicated*
Aids	Tape 8a.

Listening and writing
1 Do the spelling test as usual.

Listening and speaking
1 Spend a few minutes revising the comparative and superlative form of adjectives, concentrating on long adjectives with *more* and *the most*. Discuss *the most exciting film/sport/television programme, the most dangerous sport, the most boring subject/television programme etc.* Teach *complicated* using sums written on the board. Try to include some of the adjective forms from **WB page 58** in your revision.

Listening, speaking and reading
1 Play **TAPE 8a** while the children just listen. Ask them to explain briefly what the conversation was about.

2 **PB pages 30 and 31.** Give the children time to read the pages silently, asking for help with anything they do not understand. Play the tape again while the children follow in their books, then again while the children listen and repeat. They then practise reading the dialogue in their pairs.

3 **PB page 31.** Read aloud the questions at the bottom of the page and choose children to answer them. The children practise asking and answering the questions in their pairs.

Reading and writing
1 The children write the answers in their notebooks.

2 **WB page 58.** Read aloud the instructions to the Word Square and make sure the children understand what they have to do. While they are working, walk around to give help. The children then go on to complete the table, after you have introduced it. At the end of the lesson, the children sit in their pairs to check each other's answers.

36

Lesson Two

Aim	Consolidation of Lesson One.
New language	None.
New words	None.
Aids	Tape 8a.

Listening, speaking and writing

1   **PB pages 30 and 31.** Play **TAPE 8a** while the children follow in their books.

2   *WB page 59.* The rules for forming comparative and superlative adjectives are set out on the page. Go through the page with the class, beginning with the words that end with *y*. Look at the example already written in the box, and prompt the children to work out and tell you the rule. The children should write the normal form of the *y* adjective in the first box. Repeat with the long adjectives, then the irregular adjectives.

Pick out the *add a letter* adjectives, which are all very short (wet, sad, hot, thin, fat, flat). The others go in the regular box. Working in their pairs, the children then complete all the columns of the table, asking you for help if they are not sure.

Reading and writing

1   *WB page 60.* The children work individually, then sit in their pairs to check their answers.

Lesson Three

Aim	Consolidation.
New language	None.
New words	*advertisement, smooth, soft, tasty, crunchy, special, floating, dried*
Aids	Tape 8b. Objects to illustrate the new adjectives.

Listening and speaking

1   Teach the new adjectives with the objects and prompt the children to use them in their comparative and superlative forms.

2   Play the first advertisement on **TAPE 8b** while the children listen to see if they hear any of the new words (tastier). Ask them to tell you in their language what it is: an advertisement. Ask the children to think of similar advertisements for chocolate bars in their own language.

37

Listening, reading and speaking

1 **PB page 32.** Play the first advertisement on **TAPE 8b** again while the children look at it in their books. Play the rest of the tape while the children follow in their books, then again, while the class listens and repeats. Ask them if they can tell you any advertisements for soap in their own language. The children then read all three advertisements silently, asking for help if necessary.

Drawing and writing

1 **WB page 61.** Before the children begin, ask them to make suggestions about the kind of things they might say in their advertisements. Write some of their suggestions on the board for the children to read aloud.

2 Working in groups of four, and holding their discussions in English, the children draw and write their advertisements. If there is time, the children could work out how to present their advertisement like a television or film commercial. Let some of them present their advertisements to the class before the end of the lesson.

Lesson Four

Aim	To learn finer degrees of comparison.
New language	*a little/a little bit/a bit/a lot/much bigger/much more careful, twice as big as . . . . .*
New words	*twice, bit*
Aids	Tape 8c. Objects of various sizes for comparison.

Listening and speaking

1 Collect several books of varying sizes and lay them out in some sort of order eg big to biggest, or thick to thickest, then use them to introduce the new vocabulary in the usual way. Say *This is a big book. This is a bit bigger/a lot bigger/much bigger/twice as big as . . . . .* Repeat with *thick.* Invite children to come to the front and talk about the books using the new language.

Pretend to look inside the books for the prices and say *This one costs five pounds. It's expensive. This one costs six pounds fifty. It's a bit more expensive. This one costs ten pounds. It's much more expensive.* Continue to practise the new language with anything available in the classroom.

Listening, reading and speaking

1 **PB page 33.** Play and present the dialogue in the usual way, using **TAPE 8c**, then let the children practise reading the dialogue in their pairs. Finally, choose children to read aloud the sentences at the bottom of the page and say if they are true or false.

Reading and writing

1 **WB page 62.** Give the children time to read the sentences silently, then choose individuals to read them aloud. The children then write the correct sentences under each picture, then sit in their pairs to check their answers.

38

Lesson Five

Aim	To practise working out meanings from the context.
New language	None.
New words	To be worked out from the context.
Aids	Tape 8c. Enough dice for the class divided into groups of four.

Listening and speaking

1 **PB page 33.** Play **TAPE 8c** while the children follow in their books.

2 Explain to the children the importance of trying to work out the meaning of words they do not know by using the words they do know. Tell them that they do this instinctively in their own language, and they can do it in English as well.

3 *WB page 63.* Let the children read through the newpaper report on the right of the page, then use the multiple choice questions to help them work out the meanings. Do the first three as a class exercise, then the children complete the exercise in their pairs. They can use dictionaries (in class, in the library or at home) to check their answers.

4 *WB pages 64 and 65.* Look at the game with the children and let them read aloud the instructions. The first one of the pair to reach the finish is the winner. Give out the dice and let the children play the game in groups of four.

5 At the end of the lesson, remind the children to learn the spellings of the words in the Word Box on *WB page 63* before the next lesson.

TEST 2 (Units 5 – 8)

1 **Which word is different? Circle the different words.**

  1 check striped spotted red

  2 flight attendant pilot teacher baggage handler

  3 doctor nurse ambulance driver postman

  4 London Pakistan Egypt India

2 **Read the passage and circle the twelve words that are wrong.**
Write them correctly.

I want to complane. The dress is to small.
Its too short and to tight. It hurts my nek.
I dont like it and it's two expensive. I think
these is an terribel shop. I always come to
this shop, but I am never come here before.

_____   _____   _____   _____

_____   _____   _____   _____

_____   _____   _____   _____

3 **Read the passage, and mark the sentences** True (✓) **or** False (X).

Hello! I'm Jane Green. I'm eleven. I live in
London. I have two brothers. Bob is older
than me. He's fifteen. Tom is younger than
me. He's only five. I don't have any sisters.
  I have lots of hobbies. I like drawing and I
love riding. I hate cleaning and washing
dishes. I go to Central School. I like English
and history. I don't like maths. I love going
to the cinema and listening to pop music.
And I like playing the guitar. I am going to
learn to play the piano.

  1 Jane Green has two brothers and two sisters. ( )

  2 Jane Green's brothers are both older than she is. ( )

  3 Jane Green prefers riding to drawing. ( )

40

4 Jane Green enjoys cleaning. ( )

5 Jane Green's favourite subject is maths. ( )

6 Jane Green said that she loved watching television. ( )

7 Jane Green said that she can play the guitar and the piano. ( )

4 Circle the correct word.

1 We didn't go swimming on Tuesday so/because the water was too cold.

2 We couldn't go to the cinema because/so we watched television.

3 She was late for work so/because her car broke down.

4 He had a toothache so/because he didn't go to the concert.

5 It rains a lot in England in April because/so we didn't go on holiday then.

5 What did the teacher say to Karim? Write Karim's words.

'Karim, I am not cross with you. Your schoolwork is not bad, but you could do better. You must not waste so much time. You should always do your homework. Then your English might be as good as your maths.'

He said _____ .

He said _____ .

He said _____ .

He said _____ .

He said _____ .

6 Fill in the blanks. The first two are done for you.

fast	faster	_fastest_
amazing	_____	_____
_____	_____	hungriest
_____	_____	most exciting
_____	_____	most terrible
bad	_____	_____
sad	_____	_____
_____	_____	best

7 Fill in the blanks. Use: little twice as much

1 James is 1 metre. Mary is 2 metres. Mary is _____ tall as James.

2 Tom weighs 60 kilos. Bob weighs 59 kilos. Tom weighs a _____ more than Bob.

3 The red car costs £10,000. The blue car costs £2,000. The blue car costs _____ less than the red car.

8 Read the passage, and answer all the questions. Use sentences.

Mr Tom Green talked to our reporter about the traffic in Newtown today. He said it was terrible. All the parents were worried. They were worried that there were so many cars that travelled so fast, and an accident might happen because children play in the street.

1 Who did Mr Green talk to?

_____

2 Who did he say was worried?

_____

3 Why were they worried?

_____

_____

42

UNIT NINE

Lesson One

Aim	Revision of Present Perfect tense.
New language	None.
New words	*fallen, thrown, given, sung*
Aids	None.

Listening and writing
1 Do the spelling test in the usual way.

Listening, speaking, reading and writing
1 *WB page 66.* Discuss the pictures with the children. If you think they are capable, introduce the words *future, present, past* by translation. Do not expect the children to use these words themselves at this stage. Read aloud and have the children repeat the sentences under each picture. Let them work in their pairs to fill the blanks in the last sentences.

2 Open the door, saying at the appropriate points as you do so *I'm going to open the door. I'm opening the door. I've opened the door.* Close the door, then tell a child to repeat your action and sentences. Tell other children to close the door, open and close the window, write and draw on the blackboard in the same way. Ask the children to mime the following and say the appropriate sentences as they do so: *throw a ball, make a pancake, eat a banana.* Teach *given, sung* using the same sequence.

Reading and writing
1 Write the new words on the board for the children to practise reading and spelling.

2 *WB page 67.* Give the children time to read the sentences at the bottom of the page, then choose children to read them aloud. They then write their sentences, sit in their pairs to check them, then read them aloud. Walk around helping and checking.

3 *WB page 68.* Do this orally as a class exercise, miming or demonstrating the sequence as above wherever possible. If there is time at the end of the lesson, ask the children to make sequences of sentences using the words in the box, as in Section One.

43

Lesson Two

Aim	Consolidation.
New language	None.
New words	*wrapped, unwrapped, baked, candle, invited, blown out, set* (a table), *gone home*
Aids	Something to wrap and unwrap. A candle and matches.

Listening and speaking

1 Teach *wrapped, unwrapped, candle, blown out* by demonstration.

2 PB pages 34 and 35. Give the children time to look at the pictures and establish that this is a birthday party. Say *Look at picture one. This is Tom's mother. She has done some special things today. She has bought a present and a card. Look at picture two. She has baked a cake. Look at picture three . . . . . etc.* Describe each picture using the words on **PB page 35.** Repeat, this time prompting the class to repeat the sentences. The meanings of the other new words should be clear from the pictures. Ask questions about each picture like this. *Look at picture two. What has Tom's mother done?* to prompt the response *She has wrapped the present.* Prompt the class to ask you questions in the same way.

2 The children sit in their pairs to practise asking and answering similar questions. Tell them to ask for help if they cannot agree on the answer.

Reading, speaking and writing

1 Write the new words on the board for the children to practise reading.

2 PB page 35. Give the children time to read the sentences silently, asking for help with anything they do not understand.

3 *WB page 69.* Do this as a class exercise orally before the children, working in their pairs, write the sentences in their notebooks and then read them aloud.

Lesson Three

Aim	Consolidation.
New language	None.
New words	*fantastic, maybe, change,* (jobs), *passport*
Aids	Tape 9a. A large world map or atlases for each pair.

Listening, speaking and reading

1 Begin by asking children *Have you ever been to* (somewhere in your own country)? and prompting them to answer *Yes, I have* or *No, I haven't* or *No, I've never been to . . . . .* Ask them about some of the towns named on **PB page 36** in the same way. Point to where they are on the map.

2 Play **TAPE 9a** while the children just listen.

3 **PB page 36.** Point out that the man in uniform is the flight attendant they read about earlier (on **PB page 8**). Play the tape again while the children follow in their books. Teach the new vocabulary, then play the tape again, this time prompting the children to listen and repeat.

4 The children practise reading the dialogue in their pairs, asking for help with anything they do not understand. Demonstrate the dialogue at the bottom of the page by prompting a child to ask the questions for you to answer. Extend the practice by asking individuals similar questions about the places in the dialogue. The children then practise the questions and make up new questions and answers in their pairs.

5 *WB page 70.* Teach *passport* using the picture and if necessary, explain what a passport is and how it is stamped when you visit other countries. Say *Look at Sally's passport. Has she ever been to Hong Kong?* to prompt the response *She went in December, 1985.* Practise the other question and answer sequences in the same way and then the children practise in their pairs. At the end of the lesson, let the children guess the answer to the question at the bottom of the page.

Lesson Four

Aim	*Since* and *for* with the Present Perfect. *Ago* with the Past Simple.
New language	None.
New words	None.
Aids	Tapes 5a, 9b.

Listening, reading and speaking

1 **PB page 20.** Give the children time to look at the picture, then play **TAPE 5a** while the children listen and follow in their books.

2 **PB page 37.** Let the children look at the picture, and ask them *Who's this? What's she called?* to prompt the response *It's Sarah Martin* or *She's called Sarah Martin.* The children then close their books to listen to **TAPE 9b.** Ask a few simple questions eg *Where does Sarah live? Does she have a penfriend?*

3 **PB page 37.** Play the tape again while the children listen and follow in their books, then listen and repeat. If you think your class is capable, point out that *for* is used for lengths of time eg a week or two years, and *since* is used for a point in time, eg since Tuesday, 1990, since I was four, etc. Do not labour this point. Let the class read through the monologue again silently, and ask them to work out how old Sarah is.

45

4 Answer the questions at the bottom of the page as a class exercise, writing all the answers on the board for the children to read aloud.

Reading and writing

1 WB page 71. Working in their pairs, the children complete the first exercise, using **PB page 37** to help them. Tell them to leave a space if they are not sure of any of the answers. Choose children to read aloud their answers, and talk in more detail about any sentences which any of the children have left blank. Make sure the children's sentences are all correct.

2 WB page 71. Ask the questions around the class, letting as many children as possible answer at least one of the questions. Prompt them to answer the first six questions using *for* and *since*. When the children are answering competently, let them write the answers in their books.

Lesson Five

Aim	To write a polite invitation.
New language	None.
New words	*Atlantic, ocean, Concorde, propeller, seat*
Aids	Tape 9b.

Listening, speaking and reading

1 PB page 37. Play **TAPE 9b** while the children follow in their books.

2 WB page 71. Ask the class the questions at the bottom of the page and write some of their answers to questions 1 – 6 on the board eg *Since I was seven/1989/last week/May. For six years/two months/about a year.*

Reading and writing

1 WB page 73. The children use the table to write an invitation to their partner in their notebooks. Explain that RSVP means that the person sending the invitation would like you to answer before the day, so they know how many people are coming and how much food to prepare. When they have finished, let some of the children read aloud their invitations.

2 WB page 72. Introduce the new vocabulary for the Reading Task in the usual way, using the pictures to prompt. The children then read the passage silently, asking for help if necessary. They can then sit in pairs to complete the questions and decide on the answers before writing.

3 WB page 72. Give the children five minutes to practise the spellings in the Word Box, then give them the spelling test as usual. They can mark each other's work using the Workbook.

4 Give the children a homework task of finding out how long it takes to fly from their town (or the capital of the country) to: New York, London, Cairo, Tokyo and Singapore.

UNIT TEN

Lesson One

Aim	Revision.
New language	None.
New words	*populated, staircase, waterfall, volcano, beard, grown up, lift*
Aids	Tape 4a. Pictures to illustrate a staircase, waterfall, volcano. Tape measure.

Speaking
1 Ask the children to report on their findings about flight times to New York, London, Cairo, Tokyo and Singapore.

Listening, speaking and reading
1 **PB pages 38 and 39.** Read through the pages with the children, encouraging them to guess the meanings of the new words if possible, using the pictures only when necessary. Use these pages as a base for discussion as the children answer the questions in the text. Ask *Which teachers have a beard? Who has the longest beard? Is it as long as the beard in the picture?* Use the tape measure to show the size of things, eg a three metre waist. Encourage the children to tell you about any other biggest, highest, longest etc. records they may know about.

Reading and writing
1 Write the new words on the board for the children to read and spell.

2 Read through the first exercise on **WB page 74** and set it for homework. Children could use reference books at school and home to find the answers to the questions. They are: 1 Mount Everest; 2 Sears Tower in Chicago, USA; 3 China; 4 cheetah; 5 giant tortoise.

3 Revise qualified comparatives as in Lesson Four, Unit Eight. The children then work in their pairs to do the second exercise on **WB page 74.** When they have finished, choose children to read aloud their answers.

Listening, reading and speaking
1 **PB pages 14 and 15.** Play **TAPE 4a** while the children listen and follow in their books. Read the questions at the bottom of the page and prompt the class to answer.

47

Lesson Two

Aim	Revision.
New language	None.
New words	*puddle, yawning, cycled, neat*
Aids	Tape 10a.

Listening
1 Check the answers to the questions on **WB page 74** set for homework.

Listening, reading and speaking
1 Play **TAPE 10a** while the children listen, then ask them to explain very briefly what happened.

2 **PB page 40.** Go through the dialogue with the class, helping them to guess the meanings of the new words. Only tell them if they cannot guess. Play the tape again twice while the children follow in their Pupil's Books. Divide the class into two groups to read the two parts.

3 The children practise reading the dialogue in their pairs.

4 Practise the ask and answer sequence at the bottom of **PB page 40** with the whole class before the children practise in their pairs.

Reading and writing
1 **WB page 75.** Do several examples as a class exercise before the children begin to write the pairs of sentences in their notebooks. They can work in their pairs to help each other. At the end of the lesson, choose children to read aloud their pairs of sentences.

Lesson Three

Aim	Revision.
New language	None.
New words	*guitarist, drummer, singer, triangle, musicians*
Aids	None.

Listening, reading and speaking
1 Revise direct and reported speech as in Lessons Three and Four, Unit Six. Write a few of the pairs of sentences on the board for the children to read aloud.

48

2 WB page 76. Introduce the new words by mime and drawing and write them on the board for the children to read aloud. They then read the letter silently. Go through the letter with them, asking questions as you do so eg *Who had an argument? Who said the drummer was too slow? etc.*

Reading and writing

1 Write the new words on the board for the children to practise reading aloud.

2 WB pages 76 and 77. The children look at the picture. Ask them to point to the drummer, the guitarist, the man with the triangle, the singer, Mum, Jane and Sarah. Explain that they must write the words that were actually spoken in the speech bubbles. Do the words in the drummer's speech bubble as a class exercise and write the words on the board. The children then work in their pairs to complete, then read aloud the speech bubbles. If there is time, divide the class into groups of seven to learn and then act the dialogues at the front of the class.

Lesson Four

Aim	Revision.
New language	None.
New words	*locked, petrol, lunchtime*
Aids	Tape 10b.

Listening, speaking and reading

1 Quickly revise Present Perfect tense questions. Say *Listen carefully. Put your pen and pencils on your desks. Put your Pupil's Books under your desk. Put your Workbook under your chair.* Then ask questions like this: *Mary, have you put your pen under the chair/your Pupil's Book on your desk?* to prompt the response *Yes, I have* or *No, I haven't.*

2 PB page 41. Write the new words on the board. Ask the children to find them in the dialogue and guess their meanings. Give them five minutes, then let them guess. Help only if necessary. Then play **TAPE 10b** while the children follow in their books. Divide the class into four groups to read the four parts. Ask the children the questions at the bottom of the page, then play the tape again while the children just listen.

3 The children then practise asking and answering the questions in their pairs. They could act the dialogue in groups of four.

Reading and writing

1 WB page 78. The children write the questions, then sit in their pairs to practise asking and answering the questions with their partners.

Reading, writing and speaking

1 WB page 79. Explain what the children have to do, asking for another example of a word that goes in the column under *feet*. They can then write sentences. Ask individuals to read their completed sentences to the class.

49

Lesson Five

Aim	Test. A new song.
New language	None.
New words	*violin, flute*
Aids	Tape 10c.

Reading and writing
1　The children open **WB page 80** Explain that they are going to do a short test and that there should be no talking. Go through the instructions for question one and make sure the children understand what they have to do. When they have completed question one, do the same for the rest of the Test, question by question. The children then read through and try to improve their work. Collect in the books for marking. The points are: 1: 5; 2: 5; 3: 10; 4: 10; 5: 20; Total = 50 points.

Singing
1　Play the song on **TAPE 10c** once for the children to get the feel of it. Take them through it verse by verse, still without books. Ask them to guess the instruments, in their own language if necessary, then write the words on the board in English. As you complete each verse, have a child come to the front and draw the instrument next to the word.

2　**PB page 100.** Play the tape again all the way through while the children follow in their books, then repeat, this time asking the children to sing along in their heads. Then ask them to sing along with the tape out loud. Divide the class into five groups to sing the five verses, encouraging them to mime playing their instrument as they sing.

50

UNIT ELEVEN

Lesson One

Aim	Introduction of new language.
New language	*want* + infinitive.
New words	*Malaysia, lie, relax, countryside, water-skiing, windsurfing, monuments*
Aids	Tape 11a. Pictures to illustrate water-skiing and windsurfing.

Reading and speaking
1 Go through the marked tests on **WB pages 80-81**, helping children to understand any mistakes they made, and practising anything which has caused difficulties.

Listening and speaking
1 Draw a boy and girl on the board. Draw a 'thinks' bubble above the boy, showing a football, and over the girl, showing a plane. Say *Tom wants to be a footballer. Mary wants to be a pilot.* Repeat several times and prompt the class to repeat. Ask the class *What does Tom/Mary want to be?* Ask individual children *What do you want to be?* and prompt them to respond *I want to be a doctor/nurse/teacher/flight attendant etc.*

Listening, reading and speaking
1 Write the new words on the board and read them aloud. Play **TAPE 11a** while the children listen and then ask them a few simple questions eg *How many people are talking? What is the boy/girl called? What are they talking about?*

2 **PB pages 42 and 43.** Play the tape again, following all the usual procedures. Help the children with the new words, using the pictures. Divide the class into four groups to practise reading aloud the dialogue. Finally, play the tape again while the children listen and follow in their Pupil's Books.

3 Prompt the children to tell you things they want to do on holiday, using the new language.

Speaking and writing
1 **WB page 82.** Working in their pairs, the children follow the lines to find what each child wants to do, then write the sentences in their notebooks. At the end of the lesson, the children read aloud their sentences.

51

Lesson Two

Aim	Consolidation.
New language	None.
New words	*like to, keep fit, pushups, situps, early, bending, exercises*
Aids	Tape 11b.

Listening, reading and speaking

1 PB page 44. Play **TAPE 11b** while the children look at the picture. Discuss what the woman is doing and get a child to demonstrate *pushups, situps, bending* to teach these words and *exercises*. Go through the monologue in detail, helping the children to work out the meanings of the other new words. Play the tape again while the children listen and follow in their books, then listen and repeat. They then read the monologue silently, asking for help with anything they do not understand.

2 Ask questions eg *Do you like to keep fit/to do pushups/situps/swim? etc.* Ask *What do you like to do after school/on Fridays?* prompting the children to respond using *like to*.

3 Read aloud the questions at the bottom of the page and ask the children to say if they are true or false. The children then practise asking and answering the questions in their pairs.

Reading and writing

1 WB page 83. Let the children look at the pictures, then choose a child to read the first description aloud. Ask the class to find which picture shows what John does. When they find it, they should write *John* next to the picture. They work in their pairs to match the words and pictures and write the correct name next to each picture. Let the children read aloud their answers.

2 WB page 83. Tell the children that the girl in the picture at the bottom of the page is called Alison. The children work in their pairs to write about what she likes to do in their notebooks. Walk around helping and at the end of the lesson, choose children to read their sentences aloud.

Lesson Three

Aim	Consolidation.
New language	None.
New word	*workout, about, ant, carotene, chimpanzee, feathers, flamingo, honey, moult, penguin, pretend, shrimp, zookeeper*
Aids	Tape 11c.

52

Listening, speaking and reading
1   *WB page 82.* Ask the children questions using *What does Jack/Tony etc. want to do?* and prompt the children to respond *He wants to eat a beefburger/ watch television etc.*

2   Present the dialogue on **PB page 45** in the usual way, first as a listening comprehension, then going through it in detail. Ask the children to guess the meaning of *workout* and if necessary explain that workout means to do exercises. Play **TAPE 11c** again while the children follow in their Pupil's Books, then listen and repeat. Divide the class into two groups to read aloud the two parts. The children then practise reading aloud in their pairs.

Reading and writing
1   The children work in their pairs to make sentences from the jumbled words at the bottom of **PB page 45** and write them in their notebooks. When they have finished, choose children to write the sentences on the board for the other children to check their work.

2   *WB page 84.* Do this orally as a class exercise before the children write, then read aloud, their sentences.

3   *WB page 85.* Talk to the children briefly about the subject of the Reading Task, introducing the new vocabulary in the usual way. Give the children a few minutes to read the passage silently. Then, in their pairs, they can answer the questions, checking them aloud around the class. They might write up the answers as homework.

Lesson Four

Aim	Consolidation.
New language	None.
New words	*try to, into, mountain, break in*
Aids	None.

Drawing
1   Let several of the children draw their picture words on the board for the class to read.

Listening and speaking
1   Introduce *trying to*. Before the lesson, put a book somewhere you cannot reach it. Try to reach it and say *I'm trying to reach that book, but I can't.* Repeat this several times as you try. Choose a tall child and say *Alison, try to reach it for me, please.* As she does so, ask *What are you doing?* to prompt the response *I'm trying to reach it, but I can't.* Repeat with other children. Say to the class *Some people can touch their nose with their tongue. Try to touch your nose with your tongue.* As they try, ask children *What are you doing?* to prompt the response *I'm trying to touch my nose with my tongue* or *I'm touching my nose with my tongue.* Repeat with *Move your ears.*

53

Reading and writing

1 **WB page 86.** Use the pictures to teach *break in* and *mountain*, then write all the new words on the board for the children to read aloud. Choose children to read aloud the sentences at the bottom of the page before the children write them under the correct pictures. When they have finished, the children sit in their pairs to compare their answers, then read them aloud.

2 **WB page 87.** Do this as a class exercise before the children work in their pairs to write, then read aloud, their sentences.

Lesson Five

Aim	Listening for information.
New language	None.
New words	*shine, planet, moon, the Earth, Mercury, Mars, Saturn, Jupiter*
Aids	Tape 11d. A large picture or blackboard drawing of the Solar System.

Listening, reading and speaking

1 Working in their pairs, the children read through **PB pages 42, 43 and 45,** helping each other and asking you for help where necessary. Walk around asking questions about what they are reading.

Listening, reading and writing

1 Revise *near, nearer, nearest, this side, the other side, quarter, half*. Use the picture or blackboard drawing or, if necessary, **WB page 88,** to teach and talk about the other new words. Practise saying the names of the planets in English so the children will easily recognise them on the tape.

2 Explain that you are going to play quite a long tape and that you want them to listen very carefully, so they can write the names of the planets on the diagram. Reassure them that it doesn't matter if they don't understand everything and that you will play the tape several times. Play **TAPE 11e** while the children just listen, then repeat twice while they look at the diagram on **WB page 88.** Give them time to write in some of the names, then play the tape again so they can fill in the other names. If they ask you to play the tape yet again, do so. Then draw a rough sketch on the board and write in the names. Tell them to correct their books if they have made any mistakes.

3 Read through the True/False sentences on **WB page 88,** asking questions to ensure the children understand them. Play the tape again, telling the children to write a tick or a cross against each sentence to say if it is true or false. Let the children read aloud and correct their answers.

4 The first exercise on **WB page 89** is to help children improve their dictionary skills. They should first put the words in alphabetical order. Check they have done this correctly by choosing children to read out the words in order. Children should then look up the words in their dictionaries to check the meanings.

5 Do the spelling test on **WB page 89** in the usual way.

UNIT TWELVE

Lesson One

Aim	To use infinitives of purpose.
New language	*What for? To mend it. To make you cross.*
New word	*hardware*
Aids	Tape 12a.

Listening, speaking and reading

1   The structure of this new dialogue is very simple and repetitive, so it is ideal for both introducing and practising the new language. Introduce it in the usual way, with just listening to **TAPE 12a** first and some general comprehension questions to set the scene. At this point ask the children to try to work out the meaning of *hardware shop* and help them if necessary.

2   **PB pages 46 and 47.** Play the tape again while the children listen and follow in their books, then study the dialogue in more detail. Play the tape again while the children listen and repeat, then divide the class into two to read the two parts. Ask and answer the questions at the bottom of the page as a class exercise. Choose some children to come to the front of the class and act out the dialogue.

3   The children practise reading the dialogue in their pairs.

Writing and speaking

1   The children write, then read aloud, the questions and answers from **PB page 47** in their notebooks.

2   *WB page 90.* Ask the children about each shop, what it is called and what it sells. Then complete the first speech balloon as a class exercise. Write the sentence on the board for the children to copy. Stress the order: *to buy a book – to give to Susan*. The children then work in pairs to write the other sentences. Children then read them aloud in response to your questions: *Where is number two going? What is she going to do?*

Lesson Two

Aim	More infinitives of purpose. Revision of household words.
New language	None.
New words	None.
Aids	Household objects.

55

Listening, speaking and reading

1 Use the objects and pictures or blackboard drawings to revise all the household words on **PB page 48** and **WB page 91.** Write the words on the board for the children to practise reading aloud.

Writing

1 **WB page 91.** The children complete the picture crossword puzzle, then sit in their pairs to compare their answers, then read them aloud ie *One down, tin opener.* After each answer, say *Yes, that's right. You use it to open tins/iron clothes/comb your hair.*

Listening, reading and speaking

1 **PB page 48.** Read the page aloud, then read the first sentence for each picture and prompt the class to read the second. The children then do this in their pairs.

2 Help the children to make sentences employing the words at the bottom of **PB page 48,** using the same pattern, and write some of their sentences on the board for the class to read aloud.

Writing

1 The children sit in their pairs to help each other write sentences using all the words at the bottom of **PB page 48.** Walk around helping and checking their work. Let children read aloud their sentences before the end of the lesson.

Lesson Three

Aim	More infinitives of purpose. Revision of town vocabulary.
New language	None.
New words	None.
Aids	Tape 12b.

Listening, reading and speaking

1 **PB page 49.** Present the dialogue using **TAPE 12b**, in the usual way. If there are words the children have forgotten, encourage them to work out the meanings by themselves. Divide the class into two groups to read aloud the two parts, then let the children practise reading the dialogue in their pairs.

2 Extend the practice by talking about other buildings or shops in your town, using the same pattern of language.

Reading and writing

1 **WB pages 92 and 93.** The children write the names of the buildings under the pictures. They should leave blank any they cannot remember. They then sit in their pairs to help each other.

2 Help the children finish writing the names. Say *Look at the first picture. What is it?* Prompt a child to answer and write *1 – a cinema* on the board. Repeat with the second, third etc. picture until the children have all the names. Practise reading aloud the list of names.

3 **WB page 93.** Read aloud the first three sentences eg *You go to this building to buy bread and cakes, to catch a plane, to swim* and prompt the class to say the answer. The children write the answers, sit in their pairs to check them, then read them aloud.

Lesson Four

Aim	More infinitives of purpose.
New language	None.
New words	*whales, ducks, shell, keep warm*
Aids	Tape 12a.

Listening, speaking and reading
1 **PB pages 46 and 47.** Play **TAPE 12a** while the children listen and follow in their books, then answer the questions at the bottom of **PB page 47.**

2 Teach the new words, using the picture on **WB page 94.** Write them on the board for the children to read aloud. Ask the children to describe one of the animals without saying its name for the other children to guess eg *It can run fast. It's brown. It has a small white tail. Its back legs are longer than its front legs* (a rabbit). Give them time to think of a description, then let several of them ask the class.

Reading and writing
1 **WB page 94.** The children read both lists silently, asking for help with anything they are not sure about. Read the lists aloud while the children follow in their books. Using a pencil, the children then join words from the two lists to make sensible sentences. They check their answers in their pairs, then read their completed sentences aloud.

Listening, reading and writing
1 Revise all the prepositions on **WB page 95** by mime and demonstration. Write them on the board for the children to practise reading aloud.

2 **WB page 95.** Ask the children to talk about the picture, prompting them with questions like *What's walking on the fence/Who's sitting in front of the television? etc.* The children then complete the sentences, sit in their pairs to compare their answers, and then read their sentences aloud.

Lesson Five

Aim	To learn a new song.
New language	None.
New word	*spend*
Aids	Tapes 12b, 12c.

Listening, reading and speaking

1   PB page 49. Play **TAPE 12b** while the children listen and follow in their books. The children then read the page silently and close their books. Ask questions like this: *What's a library/stadium/cinema? etc* to prompt the response *You go there to . . . . .*

2   WB page 96. Explain to the children that they have to read the words across the page and decide which is different. In number one, for example, all four words are fruits. Three of them are round, but a banana is not. So *banana* is the odd-one-out. Tell the children that there could be more than one correct answer. The children work in their pairs, then say their answers. Any answer can be correct as long as the children have a sensible reason for saying *why* that word is the odd-one-out.

Listening and speaking

1   WB page 97. Teach the song in the usual way with **TAPE 12c**. Help the children to work out the meaning of *spend*. Encourage them to hold up the correct number of fingers as they sing each verse.

Listening and singing

1   Do the spelling test on **WB page 96** in the usual way.

TEST 3 (Units 9 – 12)

1 Fill in the blanks. The first one is done for you.

Yesterday ___*was*___ very interesting. It _____ my
birthday. I _____ late and _____ my presents. My
parents _____ me to lunch at the club. Then I _____
a party. All my friends _____ . We _____ cake and
ice cream and _____ cola.

2 Why do you go to

a library? You go there to _____ .

a stadium? You go there _____ .

a post office? You go _____ .

a hospital? You _____ .

a restaurant? _____ .

an airport? _____ .

3 Read the passage. Say whether the sentences are True (✓) **or**
False (X).

I think it's great to be healthy, so I like to keep fit and do my
workout. I get up early and always do situps and pushups and lift
weights. I think it's important to eat healthy food too. I never eat
sugar. I never drink tea or coffee. I sometimes eat meat, but I
don't eat it very often. I never go by car or bus if I can walk. I like
to swim in my lunch hour.

1 The girl who is speaking likes to keep fit and work out because
she wants to be healthy. (   )

2 She sleeps late. (   )

3 She gets out of bed, gets dressed, eats breakfast and then
leaves the house for school. (   )

4 She has sugar in her tea. (   )

5 She never eats meat. (   )

6 She plays tennis in her lunch hour. (   )

59

4 What do you use these for?

a camera? You use it to _____ .

a comb? You use it _____ .

a bridge? You use _____ .

a garage? You _____ .

a tin opener? _____ .

5 Circle the correct word.

1 Have you learned all/many your lines for the play?

2 I said the Nile was the longer/longest river in the world.

3 Have you done it never/already?

4 I want to see my present. Please wrap/unwrap it.

5 I'm going to open/opened the door.

6 Which word is different. Circle the odd-one-out.

tap   refrigerator   television   radio

waterfall   volcano   mountain   newspaper

beaches   windsurfing   swimming   waterskiing

future   present   Tuesday   past

cassette   violin   guitar   piano

train   lorry   bus   car

interesting   boring   exciting   amazing

60

7 Write sentences for the pictures. Use trying to.

_____   _____

_____

8 Read the passage. Then fill in the chart.

Tom and Mike are brothers, but they are very different.
Tom likes to play football, but Mike likes to play tennis.
Tom likes to listen to music, but Mike hates music.
Tom can drive a car, but Mike can't.
Mike likes horses. He has two. His brother doesn't like horses.

	MIKE	TOM
likes this dislikes this can can't has		

9 Circle the correct word.

1 I had a toothache so/because I went to the dentist.

2 I broke my arm so/because I went to hospital.

3 I didn't play tennis so/because it was raining.

4 We didn't go to Greece so/because it was too expensive.

5 I got up early so/because I could do my exercises.

UNIT THIRTEEN

Lesson One

Aim	Revision of question forms.
New language	None.
New words	None.
Aids	Tape 13a.

Listening, speaking and reading
1 Introduce the conversation on **PB pages 50 and 51** in the usual way. Play **TAPE 13a** while the children listen, then ask general comprehension questions. The children open their Pupil's Books. Play the tape again while the children follow in their books, then listen and repeat. Divide the class into three groups to read aloud the three parts.

2 The children read the conversation silently, asking for help with anything they do not understand. They then sit in their pairs and work together to answer the question at the bottom of **PB page 51.**

Reading and writing
1 Although the children are familiar with all the question forms used in the conversation, they have never been asked to change statements into questions. It will be necessary to do **WB page 98** as a class exercise to familiarise them with the technique. Go through the whole exercise first, giving extra examples of anything the children find difficult. When you feel that they are coping with the work, they can work in their pairs to write the questions. They should use a pencil, so they can correct their work later. Walk around helping and checking their work. At the end of the lesson, allow sufficient time to write the questions on the board so the children can check and correct their answers.

Lesson Two

Aim	Consolidation.
New language	None.
New words	*occupation, nationality, information*
Aids	Tape 13a.

Listening, reading and writing
1 **PB pages 50 and 51.** Play the **TAPE 13a** again while the children listen and follow in their books.

62

2 Ask the children to write the eleven questions in the conversation in their notebooks. They should use the Pupil's Books to help them. Choose children to read their questions aloud.

Writing
1 **WB page 99.** Teach the new words, explaining in English before you translate. Do the exercise orally before the children write, then read aloud, their questions.

Reading, speaking and writing
1 Working in their pairs, the children take turns to ask their partners the questions on **WB page 99** and fill in the form. When they have both completed the forms, they should exchange books to check each other's work.

2 **WB page 100.** Let the children think for a few minutes to decide who they would like to pretend to interview – a sports star, a politician, a singer, a film star, etc. Then children should write down as many questions as possible. They can use the suggestions given on **WB page 100** if they wish. Explain that they must write down in full the actual questions they would ask. Go round the class giving help where needed.

Lesson Three

Aim	Revision of *How* questions.
New language	None.
New words	general knowledge, *quiz, sand, team, cheetah*
Aids	None.

Reading and speaking
1 **PB page 52.** Read through the quiz questions with the children. Prompt them to try to guess the meanings of the new words and only tell them if necessary. Do not answer the questions, but make sure everyone understands them.

2 Do the quiz, either as individuals or as a team or pair effort. The answers are as follows:
Sport   11, 4 years, 10 seconds.
The World 40 000 km, 1 year, 6520 km, 70%, 8848 metres, 75°C.
Animals   170 tons, 100 kph, 6 metres, 27 metres.

Reading and writing
1 **WB page 101.** The children work in their pairs to complete the questions. They should use a pencil so they can correct their work. Walk around helping. When they have finished, go through the whole exercise, giving the children time to correct their work. Choose children to read aloud the questions, then go over their answers in pen.

2 **WB page 101.** The children find as many words in the Word Worm as they can, then sit in their pairs to help each complete the list. The words are desk, skirt, tired, red, daughter, terrible, lemon, lemonade, dentist, is, star, art, tall, all, lady.

63

Lesson Four

Aim	Consolidation.
New language	None.
New words	*spicy, Swedish, island, curry, pork, Muslim, sarong*
Aids	Tape 13b. World map. Pictures of Malaysia and Sweden.

Listening, speaking and reading
1   Show the children where Malaysia and Sweden are on the map, and tell them that they are going to read about people from these two countries. If you have been able to find pictures of the two countries, show them to the children and discuss what the weather is like there etc.

2   PB page 53. Play **TAPE 13b** while the children just listen, then ask a few simple questions eg *How many people spoke on the tape? Where are they from? Where are they now?* Then present and practise the dialogue in the usual way. There are quite a lot of new words. Encourage the children to try to work out the meanings by themselves. Divide the class into two to read the two parts, then let the children practise reading in their pairs.

3   The children sit in their pairs to practise asking and answering the questions at the bottom of the page.

Reading and writing
1   *WB page 102,* Section One. Give the children time to read both lists silently, then choose children to read them aloud. Do the first two as a class exercise, then let the children match the answers to the questions by joining them with a pencil line. They sit in their pairs to compare their answers, then choose pairs to read aloud the questions and their answers.

2   The children work by themselves to answer the questions about themselves. They can work in pairs to complete the questions at the bottom of the page. Walk around marking their work, and at the end of the lesson, let children read aloud their answers to the questions at the bottom of the page.

Lesson Five

Aim	Reading for information. Number revision.
New language	None.
New words	None.
Aids	Tape 13b.

64

Listening, reading and speaking
1 **PB page 53.** Play **TAPE 13b** while the children follow in their books. Then ask the children the same questions about their own country and any other country they know about from films or television. If you have any children from another country in your class, prompt the other children to ask him or her the same questions.

Reading and writing
1 *WB page 104.* Read aloud the questions at the bottom of the page. Explain that you are going to ask them to read something to find the answers. Tell them that it does not matter if they do not understand everything they read, but they should be able to find the answers to the questions. Give them ten minutes to read the letters on *WB pages 103 and 104* and a further five minutes to write, then read aloud their answers.

Listening and writing
1 *WB page 105.* Play number bingo in the usual way. Make sure to make a note of the numbers you called in case there is a dispute. Let a child call the numbers for the second game.

2 Do the spelling test in the usual way.

Reading and speaking
1 There should be time at the end of the lesson for the children, working in their pairs, to read through Unit Seven in their Pupil's Book, asking you for help with anything they cannot read or understand. Walk around asking questions about what they are reading.

65

UNIT FOURTEEN

Lesson One

Aim	To ask negative questions.
New language	*Isn't that John? Didn't you see him? Don't you like it? Haven't you seen him?*
New words	*marine, killer, gallons, seals, otters, deer, bored, Hawaiian, canoes, scared, tunnel, shark, snapshots, million*
Aids	Tape 14a. Pictures to illustrate the new words.

Listening and speaking

1 There is a great deal of new vocabulary in this dialogue, some of which it is not easy to work out from context. Introduce some of the new words with the pictures, taking the opportunity to discuss marine parks in general and also some of the animals you can see there. Then play **TAPE 14a** while the children listen, and then answer a few simple comprehension questions.

Listening, speaking and reading

1 **PB pages 54 and 55.** Let the children look at the pictures and point out the dolphins and the killer whale. Play the tape again while the children follow in their books, then go through the dialogue, helping the children to work out the meanings of the new words. Some can be explained in English eg *snapshot* – photograph, *million* – a thousand thousand. Continue in the normal way with the class dividing into groups to read the two parts and the children practising in their pairs. Finally, play the tape again while the children just listen.

2 Ask the children to find and read aloud any questions in the dialogue, and write them on the board for the whole class to read aloud. They are all negative questions. These are asked if you are almost sure that you know the answer. If you feel your children are capable, you can tell them this, but do not labour the point.

3 Read aloud the questions at the bottom of the page, then give the children time to read silently to find the answers. Then say them.

Reading and writing

1 **WB page 106.** Go through the first exercise orally with the children. Encourage them to look for clues in the sentences to find which word is missing. For example, *last Saturday* shows that they must use a past tense word. Do not be too technical at this stage. Encourage the children to look again at the dialogue if they are stuck. Let them work in their pairs to complete the exercise, then read aloud their answers. Write the correct answers on the board so the children can correct their work.

66

2 WB page 106. The children complete the second exercise by themselves. They can use the Pupil's Book to help them. Walk around helping and checking their work. The children then sit in their pairs to ask each other their questions.

Lesson Two

Aim	Consolidation.
New language	None.
New words	None.
Aids	Tape 14a. Pictures from Lesson One.

Listening, reading and speaking
1 Briefly revise all the new words as in Lesson One.

2 PB pages 54 and 55. Play **TAPE 14a** while the children listen and follow in their books.

Reading and writing
1 WB page 107. Look at the first exercise with the children. Help them to find the clue in each sentence which tells them how to complete the question, then help them say the correct question. The children then work in their pairs to write, then read aloud their questions.

2 WB page 107. The children complete the second exercise, using the Pupil's Book to help them if they wish. Give them time to finish, then let them read aloud their answers and translate each one into their own language to check for understanding.

3 Tell the children they are going to do a memory test. They are going to look at a picture for three minutes, then they have to cover the picture and write down as many things as they can remember, in English.

4 WB page 108. Run through the English words for the things in the picture, then give them three minutes to look at it. They then cover the picture with their Pupil's Books, and write as many words as they can remember. When they have all finished, ask if anybody has written twenty words. Praise anybody who has, then give them one more minute to look at the picture before they cover it again and try to write the rest of the words. Then let them complete their lists by looking at the picture, and then exchange books with their partners to check each other's work.

Lesson Three

Aim	Reading comprehension.
New language	None.
New words	*kitten, clear* (eyes), *basket, fresh*
Aids	None.

67

Listening, speaking and reading

1 PB page 57. Read through the information leaflet with the children, helping them to work out the meanings of the new words from the context or from clues in the pictures. When you feel they understand it, read through it again while the children follow in their books. Ask the children if any of them have a cat, and let them tell the class where they bought it and how they look after it. Choose children to read aloud and answer the questions at the bottom of the page.

Reading and writing

1 *WB page 109*. Read through the instructions and check that the children understand. Help them decide which should be the first sentence, then let them try to put the other sentences into the correct order, then sit in their pairs to compare and discuss their answers. The children then read the sentences in the correct order around the class.

2 *WB page 107*. Look at the pictures and check the children understand each stage. Then, working in pairs, the children write eight sentences to explain how to make a banana split. Help them with the first sentence: *Before you start, wash* . . .

Lesson Four

Aim	Consolidation.
New language	*Why haven't you cleaned your room?*
New words	None.
Aids	Tapes 14a, 14b.

Listening, speaking and reading

1 The children sit in their pairs to read through the dialogue on **PB page 55,** asking for help with anything they cannot read or understand. Play **TAPE 14a** while they listen and follow in their books.

2 Ask the children to tell you, in English, everything they can remember about how you keep a kitten. Prompt the children to tell the class any bad things their kittens have done eg *My kitten ate my mother's shoes etc.*

3 Present **TAPE 14b** and the dialogue on **PB page 56** in the usual way, having first looked carefully at the picture and then closed books to listen to the tape for the first run through. After the children have practised reading the dialogue in their pairs, have the children extend the dialogue by using other clues in the picture. Write some of their questions and answers on the board for the class to read aloud.

Reading and writing

1 *WB page 110.* Go through this exercise orally with the children. Help them to find the clues which tell them which word to use. Remind them that we use questions like this when we think we already know the answer. The children, working in their pairs, then write their answers in pencil so they can correct them if they make mistakes. Give them plenty of time to discuss their answers, then choose children to read them aloud. Write the correct answers on the board so the children can correct their work, and if there is time, rewrite their answers in pen.

Lesson Five

Aim	To write a letter.
New language	*Best Wishes.*
New word	*wishes, sauce, nuts, chopped, spoonful*
Aids	Tape 14c.

Listening and speaking

1 *WB page 111.* Play the rhymes, **TAPE 14c**, one at a time, for the children to discuss and then repeat. Help them to work out any new words from the context or picture clues.

Reading and writing

1 *WB page 33.* The children read through the International Penfriend Club form they filled in some time ago.

2 *WB page 112.* Explain to the children that this is a letter from someone who filled in the same form. Let the children try to read through it silently, asking for help with anything they do not understand. When they have all finished, explain that *Best Wishes* is a polite way of ending a letter. Go through the letter in more detail with the children.

The children then write a letter to Faisal. Show them how to begin with *Thank you for your letter.* Discuss some of the language they might want to use eg *I don't like Science very much* or *I don't have a horse, but I would love to have one etc.* Walk around while they are working, helping and checking their work. At the end of the lesson, let some of the children read their letters aloud.

3 Remind the children to learn the words in the Word Box on ***WB page 111*** for the spelling test next lesson.

69

UNIT FIFTEEN

Lesson One

Aim	Revision.
New language	None.
New words	*pass, exams, medicine, study*
Aids	None.

Listening, reading and speaking
1 Do the spelling test in the usual way.

2 PB page 58. Remind the children of the difference between *like* and *prefer*, then read and discuss the statements made by the three children. Ask and answer questions about the three monologues. Ask the children the questions at the bottom of the page before the children practise in their pairs.

3 PB page 59. Follow the same procedures with the conversation on this page. Make sure the children understand the difference between *I'm doing my homework* and *I'm trying to do my homework*. Let the children practise reading the conversation in groups of four. Ask the class the questions at the bottom of the page before the children practise in their pairs. Choose a group of four children to act out the dialogue in front of the class.

Reading and writing
1 *WB page 114,* Section One. Ask the children to make sentences from the Sentence Box before they begin to write. If a child makes a wrong sentence, write it on the board and prompt the class to say why it is wrong, or explain yourself if necessary. The children then write the ten sentences, and sit in their pairs to compare and check each other's work.

2 *WB page 114*. Go through the second exercise orally before the children write, then read aloud their answers.

Lesson Two

Aim	Revision.
New language	None.
New words	None.
Aids	Tape 15a.

70

Reading and writing

1 *WB page 115.* Choose children to read aloud the questions at the top of the page. The children then complete the questions. Remind them to look for clues to help them write the correct words. When they have finished, check the answers around the class.

2 *WB page 116.* Look at the picture and prompt the children to say true sentences about it. The children then write their questions. Walk around correcting any mistakes, then choose children to read their questions aloud for the class to answer. The children then practise asking and answering each other's questions in their pairs. Check these around the class.

Lesson Three

Aim	Revision. A listening exercise.
New language	None.
New words	*Eskimo, igloo, oil company, frozen, sleigh, hunt, Arctic*
Aids	Tape 15a. World map.

Reading, speaking and writing

1 PB page 60. Introduce, discuss and practise the passage in the usual way. Show the children where the Arctic is on the map. Do the true or false exercise at the bottom of the page. Ask the children to tell you anything else they know about Eskimos. The children then read through the passage silently, asking for help with anything they are still not sure about. The children then work in their pairs to read aloud the sentences at the bottom of the page and say if they are true or false.

2 *WB page 117.* Do the first exercise orally before the children write their questions, sit in their pairs to check them, then read them aloud around the class.

Listening and writing

1 Prepare for **TAPE 15a**, which is a listening exercise in which the children listen carefully for the word which is stressed. Explain *stressed* and practise several sentences as a class exercise. Say for example *Don't you LIKE learning English?/It's not yours. It's MINE./I said come at TEN o'clock.* When they can do this, tell them to close their eyes while you say other sentences. It is more difficult when you cannot see the person who is speaking. Use sentences like this: *Don't YOU like football? Don't you like FOOTBALL? Can't you speak ENGLISH? Isn't MARY your sister? etc.*

2 Play **TAPE 15a** question by question, and prompt the children to call out the word which they think is stressed. Repeat, this time with the children looking at the second exercise on **WB page 117** and circling the stressed words. Let them read out the stressed words around the class so the children can correct any mistakes. The class then reads aloud the questions, stressing the words they have circled.

71

Lesson Four

Aim	Revision. A listening exercise.
New language	None.
New words	*type, immediately, boss, test*
Aids	Tapes 15b.

Writing
1 *WB page 118*.Go through the first exercise orally before the children write the answers, sit in their pairs to check them, then read their questions and answers aloud.

Listening, speaking and reading
1 Present and practise the dialogue on **PB page 61** with **TAPE 15b** in the usual way. The children read the dialogue aloud in two groups, then the children practise it in their pairs.

Writing
1 *WB page 118*. The children complete the second exercise, using their Pupil's Books to help them, sit in their pairs to compare and check their answers, then read their completed sentences aloud around the class.

2 *WB page 119*. The children complete the picture crossword. Walk around helping and checking their work.

Lesson Five

Aim	Practice Test.
New language	None.
New words	None.
Aids	None.

Reading and writing
1 The children open ***WB page 120***. Explain that they are going to do a short test and that there should be no talking. Go through the instructions for question one and make sure the children understand what they have to do. When they have completed question one, do the same for the rest of the Test, question by question. The children then read through and try to improve their work. Collect in the books for marking. The points are: 1: 5; 2: 10; 3: 5; 4: 10; 5: 20. Total = 50 points.

72

UNIT SIXTEEN

Lesson One

Aim	To learn the Past Continuous tense.
New language	*Was the sun shining? Were the monkeys fighting?*
New words	None.
Aids	None.

Reading and speaking
1 Go through the marked tests in the Workbooks, helping children to understand any mistakes they made, and practising anything which has caused difficulties.

Listening, reading and speaking
1 Introduce the new language. Mime writing on the board, then say several times *What was I doing? I was writing.* Call out a child and whisper to her to mime writing. Tell the class they must not guess until she has finished. Let her mime, then say to the class several times *What was she doing? She was writing.* Ask the class, then individuals the question and prompt them to answer. Repeat with two children miming drawing, and *What were they doing? They were drawing.*

2 **PB pages 62 and 63.** Look at the picture and discuss it very thoroughly, asking the children to make sentences about it and ask quite probing questions about the details. Ask and prompt the children to answer the questions at the bottom of **PB page 63** before the children practise asking and answering them in their pairs.

3 Tell the children that they must remember as much as they can about the picture. Give them three minutes to look and try to remember. They then shut their books.

4 Tell the children what you remember about the picture using the patterns *A man/woman/panda was . . . . . ing. The monkeys were . . . . . ing.* Prompt them to make similar sentences about what they remember.

5 *WB page 122,* Section One. Read aloud the questions at the top of the page, then choose children to read them aloud and answer them. When they answer *Yes* or *No,* prompt them to expand their answers to *Yes, it was/they were* or *No, it wasn't/they weren't etc.* The children then practise asking and answering the questions in their pairs.

Writing
1 *WB page 122,* Section Two. The children write as many sentences as they can without looking at their Pupil's Books. Ten minutes before the end of the lesson, they can open their books and check if their sentences are correct before reading them aloud around the class.

73

2 WB page 122. The children work on this dictionary task in the usual way: putting the words in order, checking them orally and then looking them up.

Lesson Two

Aim	Consolidation.
New language	None.
New word	*fireworks*
Aids	Teaching clock.

Listening, reading and speaking
1   Revise telling the time with the teaching clock, then ask questions around the class eg *What time did you get up/go to bed last night/arrive at school/begin this lesson? What time did you have lunch/breakfast? What time does school begin/end every day? etc.*

2 WB page 123, Section One. The children draw lines to match the clock faces to the written times, then sit in their pairs to compare and correct their answers.

3 WB page 123, Section Two. Children should work individually to write answers to the questions. Choose children to read aloud their answers to the class.

Reading and writing
1   **WB page 124**, Section One. Children draw the hands on the clocks to show the correct time. Use a teaching clock to show the correct answers when they have finished.

2 WB page 124, Section One. Go through the exercise orally as revision before the children write, then read aloud and correct their answers.

3 WB page 125. Invite the children to make sentences using the pictures and words. Make sure they say sentences beginning with all the words in the box on the left, to make sure they remember *I/he/she/it was. They/you/we were.* The children write and then read aloud their sentences around the class. No sentence should be repeated as they read.

Lesson Three

Aim	Consolidation.
New language	None.
New word	*secretary*
Aids	Tape 16a.

Listening, speaking and reading

1 Present and practise **PB page 64** and **TAPE 16a** in the usual way. Explain the difference between a *secretary* and a *typist*. A secretary is involved in more jobs around the office than just typing.

2 The children make sentences as instructed at the bottom of **PB page 64.** Note that the nine people are the cleaning lady and eight children. The children should do this orally.

Reading and writing

1 *WB page 126,* Section One. Help the children compose the questions, then let them sit in their pairs to practise asking and answering the questions. Walk around helping and checking.

2 *WB page 126,* Section Two. Make sure the children all understand *rhyme*. Give them several pairs of examples and write them on the board for the children to read. Include some examples where the spelling is different, but the words rhyme, for example *bed, said* or *two, blue,* and words with the same spelling which do not rhyme eg *blow, now*. Discuss all the words in the exercise, and have the children practise their pronunciation. The children then sit in their pairs to find, then read aloud, the pairs of words.

Lesson Four

Aim	Consolidation.
New language	*While X was . . . . .ing, Y was . . . . .ing.*
New word	*siesta*
Aids	Tape 16b.

Listening, reading and speaking

1 **PB page 65** and **TAPE 16b.** Present and practise the dialogues in the usual way. Divide the class into three to practise reading aloud the three parts. Choose children to read aloud and answer the questions at the bottom of the page. Children can act the dialogue in groups of three.

Reading and writing

1 *WB page 127.* Establish that these are the same people you have just been reading about. Give the children time to look at the pictures and read the first sentence, then read the sentence aloud and prompt the children to repeat it. Do the second sentence as a class exercise, then let the children sit in their pairs to make up and then say the other sentences. They then write the sentences in their notebooks, sit in their pairs to compare their answers, then finally read their sentences aloud.

75

Lesson Five

Aim	Listening comprehension.
New language	None.
New words	*petrol pump, tyre, car wash, mechanic, map, windscreen, roofrack*
Aids	Tapes 16c, 16d, 16e, 16f.

Listening, speaking and reading
1 The tongue twisters and rhymes on **WB page 128** are just for fun and to practise some complicated English sounds. Begin with the tongue twister. Play **TAPE 16c** several times while the children follow in their books, then prompt the whole class, then individuals to say the sentences.

Listening
1 This is a listening exercise in which children have to listen for the sound *b* at the beginning of words. Do a few examples orally from the tape before you play it. Play **TAPE 16d** through once while the children listen very carefully, then again while they tick on **WB page 128** the words which begin with *b*. Play the tape again so they can check their work.

2 In the second listening exercise, children have to listen to five pairs of words and say whether the words in each pair are the same or different. Play **TAPE 16e** through once while the children listen, then again while they tick the correct answers on **PB page 128**. Play the tape again so they can check their work.

Listening, speaking and colouring
1 **WB page 129.** Introduce and practise all the new words using the picture. To make it more fun, give the children commands to find and colour various objects on the page. Say *Can you see Dave's windscreen? Can you find it? Colour it blue.* Repeat for all the other new words. Tell the children to colour all the objects a different colour so you can extend the practice by asking *What's blue/red etc.* Further extend the practice by asking questions about the picture using the new language eg *What's on the roofrack? How many petrol pumps can you see? Who is using the petrol pumps? What is the mechanic doing? etc.*

2 Tell the children that they are going to listen to a tape of Dave (the man in the picture) telling his wife what happened at the garage. If they hear any mistakes, they must put a cross on the appropriate place in the picture. Play **TAPE 16f** twice so they can pick out one or two obvious mistakes, and show them how to mark the picture with a cross. Play the tape again several times so the children can find all the mistakes.

3 Finish the lesson with the spelling test (**WB page 128**) as usual.

76

TEST 4 (Units 13 – 16)

1 Change these sentences into questions.

Example: We saw the new Stevie Spellbound film.
Have you seen the new Stevie Spellbound film?

1 I would like a beefburger and a cola.

_____

2 We are going to the cinema tonight.

_____

3 Sally has been to London.

_____

4 I've been asleep since 9 o'clock.

_____

5 They have been watching television all afternoon.

_____

6 He has broken the cup.

_____

2 Fill in the blanks.

1 _____ high is the mountain?

2 _____ do you begin school?

3 _____ did you put my book?

4 _____ coat is this?

5 _____ do you prefer, Greece or Turkey?

6 _____ are you so late?

7 _____ time are we going to have the barbecue?

8 _____ has both brothers and sisters?

3 Write a letter to a penfriend. Ask:

What time he/she goes to school. How he/she travels to and from school. How long does the journey take. His/her favourite subject. What he/she likes to do on holiday.

Dear Penfriend,

_____

_____

_____

_____

_____

_____

_____

Best wishes

4 Fill in the blanks. Use | Isn't Haven't Wasn't Didn't Doesn't

1 _____ London in England?

2 _____ the concert good last night?

3 _____ you heard the news?

4 _____ you do your homework yesterday?

5 _____ she know how to speak German?

5 Circle the correct word.

1 Tom was playing football while/after John was reading and Nadia was getting up.

2 She studied English when/before she studied German.

3 After/While the concert, we went to a restaurant.

4 She could talk while/before she was one year old.

5 While/When are we going to eat dinner?

78

6 Fill in the blanks. Use: in at on

1 I always watch television _____ Friday nights.

2 The football match starts _____ 2.30.

3 I'm going to go _____ holiday _____ July.

4 It's cold _____ December _____ Canada.

5 I go to bed _____ 9.30.

7 Write true answers about yourself.

1 What is your favourite television programme?
2 Which subject do you like most?
3 How do you come to school?
4 Who is your favourite film star?
5 Where did you go on your last holiday?
6 What do you want to be when you grow up?

8 Fill in the blanks using the word in brackets to help you.

1 Where _____ you _____ this evening? (go)

2 _____ you _____ English? (speak)

3 When _____ you _____ the exercise? (finish)

4 _____ you ever _____ Luxor? (visit)

5 _____ you _____ football on Friday? (play)

6 _____ you _____ a biscuit? (eat)

UNIT SEVENTEEN

Lesson One

Aim	To contrast the Past Simple and Past Continuous tenses.
New language	None.
New words	*reception, bracelet, thief, maid, waiter, guest*
Aids	Tape 17a.

Listening and speaking

1   PB page 66. The children look at the picture of the hotel and the guests there. Discuss what everybody is doing and use the picture to introduce and practise the new words. Then tell the children that the picture shows what was happening *last night*. Help them to make sentences using the new vocabulary and the Past Continuous tense eg *The woman in Room 15 was reading. The maid was cleaning Room 8 etc.*

2   Go back to look again at Room 12 and establish that something has been stolen and the police are trying to find out who the thief was. It is very important that everybody in the hotel can say exactly what they were doing at the time of the theft. Then play **TAPE 17a** and work on it in the usual way. Talk about how police investigate a crime, finding out what time it took place and then questioning all the people who might have done it. If you think that your pupils are capable of understanding, point out the use of the Past Simple for the actions known and completed at the time of the crime, and the use of the Past Continuous for actions still going on at the time of the crime. Have the class read the dialogue in two groups, then let the children practise reading it in their pairs. They should take turns to be the manager and the policewoman.

3   The children work in their pairs to make up and answer the questions the policewoman asked the people in Rooms 15, 11, 7 and 3. Choose pairs of children to act their dialogues in front of the class.

Speaking and writing

1   WB page 130. Go through the exercise orally with the children, making sure they answer using the pattern *The woman/man was . . . . . ing.* The children then write their answers, sit in their pairs to compare and check them, then read their sentences aloud. Then practise asking the class questions like this: *What was X doing when the thief stole the bracelet?* to prompt the response *When the thief stole the bracelet, X was . . . . . ing.*

80

Lesson Two

Aim	Consolidation.
New language	None.
New words	None.
Aids	Tape 17a.

Listening, reading and speaking

1 Write the new words from Lesson One on the board for the children to read aloud. Play **TAPE 17a** again while the children listen and follow on **PB page 67**. They then read through the dialogue silently, asking for help with anything they are not sure about. In their pairs, children ask each other questions about what the people in the hotel were doing at 10:30, using the picture on **PB page 66** and the dialogue on **PB page 67** to help them.

Speaking and writing

1 *WB page 131.* Remind the children that the people are Mother, Mike and Alison. Do the exercise orally, making two sentences for each picture like the ones at the top of the page. The children write their pairs of sentences in their notebooks, sit in their pairs to check them, then read them aloud around the class.

2 *WB page 132.* Each child first chooses and then writes the name of the character, then reads the list of activities. They then draw lines between the times and the activities, taking care that the time and the activity fit eg eating lunch at eight-thirty would not be sensible. Every child's Workbook should be different.

3 The children then sit in their pairs to practise asking each other *What was (name) doing at half past seven yesterday?*

Lesson Three

Aim	Revision of occupations vocabulary.
New language	None.
New words	*builder, tailor*
Aids	None.

Listening and speaking

1 Ask the children to tell you all the names of the jobs in English that they know. Remind them of the new words they learned in Lesson One. As each child says a job, call her out to write the word on the board. Let the class check the spelling and correct it if necessary. Make sure these words are included, prompting the children if necessary: *dentist, painter, butcher, singer, mechanic, farmer, nurse, waiter, guitarist.* Let the children mime all the jobs for the class to guess.

2   Introduce and practise the new words in the usual way.

3   Ask several children to say what their parents' jobs are and what they would like to be when they grow up.

Reading and writing
1   Add the new words to the list on the board and have the children practise reading them aloud.

2   *WB page 133.* Give the children time to look at the pictures and then say the various occupations while the children point to the correct picture.

3   The children complete the picture puzzle, then sit in their pairs to check their work and then read aloud the answers around the class. Finally ask the class *What is the job in the box?*

Lesson Four

Aim	Revision.
New language	None.
New words	*waitress, junior*
Aids	Tape 17b.

Reading and writing
1   *WB page 134.* Go through the form with the children, asking them to work out the meanings of the new words. Then read through the whole form while the children listen and follow in their books. The children then read silently, asking for help with anything they are not sure about. Go through the questions and answers orally before the children write the answers in their notebooks, sit in their pairs to compare, then read their answers aloud.

2   *WB page 136.* The children fill in the Memory Quiz without looking at *WB page 134.* They then sit in their pairs to check each other's answers by looking at *WB page 134.*

3   The children work in their pairs to make three new sentences about Carol, then read them aloud around the class.

Listening, speaking and reading
1   **PB pages 68 and 69** and **TAPE 17b**. Introduce and practise in the usual way.

2   Play a game. Working around the class, each child says a job description eg *I look after people's teeth/paint houses/build houses etc.* and the class says *You're a dentist/painter/builder etc.* The children then practise the game in their pairs. Extend this by having children say *I'm a dentist/painter/baker etc. What do I do?* and prompting the class to respond *You look after people's teeth/paint houses/build houses etc.*

3   The children practise asking the same questions and answers in their pairs.

82

Lesson Five

Aim	A speaking task.
New language	None.
New words	None.
Aids	Tape 17b. A piece of paper and some paste.

Listening, speaking and reading
1   PB pages 68 and 69. Play **TAPE 17b**.

2   PB page 69. Help the children to say what the people in the pictures at the bottom of the page do.

Speaking
1 The speaking task on **WB pages 135 and 136** is designed to encourage a pair of children to find out a story by asking each other questions. The first child in each pair opens the Workbook at page 135, and the second child at page 136. They should **not** look at the other's page. Each child has half a story and they must ask each other questions until they both know the whole story. Give them time to complete the exercise, then choose children to tell the class everything that happened on 'The Terrible Day'.

Writing
1 When the children are confident about the events of the story, and they have heard a few children tell the story to the class, the children should write the story on **WB page 137**. Explain that their stories can be short, but that they should include all the events of 'The Terrible Day', as shown in the six pictures.

Reading and writing
1   WB page 137. The children sit in pairs to work out how to complete the table. Choose children to tell the class where each person works and what they do. The children can then complete the tables in their own books.

2 Finish the lesson with the spelling test in the usual way.

UNIT EIGHTEEN

Lesson One

Aim	Revision.
New language	None.
New words	*describe, description, straight, curly, eyebrows, crazy, mean, fit*
Aids	None.

Listening, speaking and reading

1 PB page 70. Read aloud the words at the top of the page, then talk about the four 'Wanted' posters, describing them using the new words and revising other clothes and personal vocabulary. Invite the children to describe them. Write the new words on the board for the children to read aloud and spell.

2 Ask the children to read the description under the first picture silently, asking for help with anything they do not understand. Then you read it aloud, and ask the class which poster it describes. Repeat with the other three descriptions.

Reading, speaking and writing

1 *WB page 138.* Explain to the children that they are going to *describe* the man in the picture. First they will look carefully at the man, then they will choose the right words, finally they will write their own *descriptions*. Read the passage, asking the children to choose the right words as you read along. They are: *young, twenty, tall, thin, short, straight, dark, square, large, small, thick, dark, beard, striped, jeans, black, smart, clean.*

2 The children then write their own descriptions of the man.

Lesson Two

Aim	Revision and consolidation of adjectives.
New language	None.
New words	None.
Aids	None.

Listening and speaking

1 Revise the idea of opposites by asking the children to say some opposites in their own language. Then let the children say any opposite they know in English eg *happy/sad, black/white.* Write their opposites in a list on the board.

84

Listening, speaking and writing

1   *WB page 139.* Give the children time to look at the page, then ask for volunteers to tell you the first three opposites. Add these to the list on the board, then prompt the children to circle *good, white, heavy* in the Word Square. The children then work in their pairs to write as many of the opposites as they can and find and circle the words in the Word Square. When most of them have finished, call out children to add their pairs of opposites to the list on the board, and if there are any opposites which the children have not found, help them and give them clues until they guess it correctly. Give the children time to correct and complete their work from the list on the blackboard.

2   *WB page 140.* Read aloud the sentence at the top of the page and discuss, in the children's own language, how this is a very good description. Write *as white as snow* on the blackboard for the children to read aloud. Directly underneath write *as black as* . . . . . and prompt the children to finish the simile with any English word that makes a good description. Complete the exercise orally before the children write, then read aloud their similes. The children then make up and write some similes of their own, then read them aloud around the class. Emphasise that there are no *correct* answers.

Lesson Three

Aim	Revision and consolidation of adjectives.
New language	None.
New words	useful, ear-rings
Aids	Tape 18a.

Listening, reading and speaking

1   PB page 72 and **TAPE 18a.** Present and practise the dialogue in the usual way, first the class and then pairs reading the two parts aloud.

Reading and writing

1   *WB page 141.* The children have already encountered the ordering adjectives in an informal way and have read and talked about *small square red sweets etc.* Do not expect the children to *learn* these categories at this stage. They should make phrases from the table orally, then write four of them in their Workbooks. They do not need to use a word from every column, but however many they use, they should be in the same order as they are in the table.

2   The children write out the mixed up sentences in the correct order, then sit in their pairs to compare their answers before reading them aloud.

3   Finally, children could add other words to the table – such as more colours, more patterns (refer them to ***WB page 43***), more opinions, more shapes.

Lesson Four

Aim	Revision and consolidation of adjectives.
New language	Verbs of the senses plus adjectives. *This looks good. This tastes strange.*
New words	*taste, smell, look, sauce, recipe*
Aids	Tape 18b.

Listening, speaking and reading

1 Revise *eyes, tongue, nose, ears, fingers, mouth* and what you do with them ie *see, feel, taste, smell, hear, speak etc.* Talk about things that smell or taste good or bad.

2 **PB page 73** and **TAPE 18b**. Present and practise the dialogue in the usual way, discussing new vocabulary and having the children practise the dialogue in their pairs. Pairs of children can come to the front of the class and act out the dialogue.

3 *WB page 142.* Choose children to read aloud the sentences at the top of the page and mime their meanings. Repeat, with a different child miming and the class reading the sentences aloud.

4 Children stand up and mime any of the sentences for the class to guess.

Writing

1 *WB page 142.* The children write the sentences under the correct pictures, then sit in their pairs to compare their answers before reading them aloud around the class.

2 *WB page 143.* Do the first two orally, then let the children work in their pairs and read aloud their sentences at the end of the lesson.

Lesson Five

Aim	Reading skills practice.
New language	None.
New words	*mice, shell, shore*
Aids	Tapes 18c, 18d.

Listening, reading and speaking

1 *WB page 144.* Read aloud the first tongue twister, or play **TAPE 18c**, and prompt the class to repeat it slowly, then faster and faster. Ask individuals to say it as fast as they can. Repeat with the second tongue twister.

86

2   WB page 144. The children practise the sound of *b* and *v* in words they already know. Write some of the words (*black, brown, very, violin, volcano, big, ball etc.*) on the board for the children to practise saying aloud. Say some of the words and prompt the children to tell you if they begin with *b* or *v*.

To help the children, show them how the two sounds are made. *B* is made with the lips together and *v* is made with the top teeth and bottom lip. Read the list again, this time with the children watching your lips as you speak, and again, this time with the children having their eyes closed.

3   Play **TAPE 18d** once while the children just listen. Tell them what to do. They then look at **WB page 144** and write the letters in the boxes as you play the tape. Repeat, so they can check before they read aloud their answers.

Reading
1   WB page 145. Read aloud and discuss the story, prompting the children to guess the meaning of the new words. The children then read the questions and circle the correct answers. They should sit in their pairs to compare their answers before they read them aloud around the class.

2   Finish the lesson with the spelling test.

UNIT NINETEEN

Lesson One

Aim	To introduce adjectives beginning with *un*.
New language	None.
New words	*unmarried, rowing boat, uncertain, unsure, wise, unwise, unsafe, unhurt, unexciting, unwell, unhappy, unhealthy, uncombed, untidy, uninteresting, unlike, kind, unkind, unpatterned*
Aids	Tape 19a.

Listening, reading and speaking
1 PB pages 74 and 75 and **TAPE 19a**. Teach *wise* and *kind* by translation before you begin. Present and practise the newspaper articles, one at a time, in the usual way. Discuss how *un* in front of an adjective makes it an opposite. Prompt the children to think of different ways to say *unhappy, unwell, uninteresting* (sad, ill, boring).

2 The children read through all the articles in their pairs, asking for help with anything they are not sure about. Ask and answer the questions at the bottom of **PB page 75** as a class exercise before the children practise them in their pairs.

Reading and writing
1 *WB page 146.* Do the matching exercise orally before the children draw the lines.

Reading, speaking and writing
1 *WB page 146*. The children read the three 'letters' silently first. Then they decide which words to use to replace the underlined words. Move around the class and give help where necessary. Finally ask individual children to read the 'letters' aloud using the new words.

Lesson Two

Aim	Consolidation of Lesson One.
New language	None.
New words	*comfortable, uncomfortable*
Aids	Tape 19a.

Listening, reading and speaking
1 PB pages 74 and 75. Play **TAPE 19a** all the way through while the children just listen, then repeat while they follow in their books. Give the class time to read the articles silently, then ask the questions at the bottom of **PB page 75.**

Reading and writing
1 *WB page 147.* Do this as a class exercise before the children write, then read aloud their answers.

Reading, speaking and writing
1 *WB page 89*. First check through the words in the Reading Task which might give difficulty, although the children have already met them: *fashion designer, terrific, customers, millionaires, successful, jet-set, relax*. Then give the children a few minutes to read the text silently. Move around the class to give help where necessary.

2 Working in pairs, the children have a few minutes to answer the questions. Then ask individual children to read the answers aloud.

3 Continuing in pairs, the children choose the words to describe Paul's life. Finally ask around the class for words about his life, house and clothes.

Lesson Three

Aim	Consolidation and extension.
New language	None.
New words	*rubbish bin, perfume, roll, unroll, screw, unscrew, button, unbutton*
Aids	Tape 19b.

Listening, reading, speaking and writing
1 *WB page 149.* Use the pictures to revise known words and to teach the new verbs. Mime the verbs for the class to guess, then let children mime for you to guess.

2 Write the words at the top of **WB page 149** on the board for the class to read aloud and spell, then point to the words in random order and prompt the class to mime the action. The children then write the correct words under the pictures and sit in their pairs to check their answers before they read them aloud around the class.

3 PB page 76 and **TAPE 19b**. Play the tape first while the children just listen, and try to work out what is happening. The children then turn to **PB page 76.** Play the tape again, following all the usual procedures. Divide the class into four groups to read aloud the four parts.

89

4 *WB page 150.* Give the children time to read silently the two lists at the top of the page. Show the class *a button* and demonstrate *button* and *unbutton*. The children match the words in the two lists by drawing lines in pencil, using **PB page 76** to help them, then sitting in their pairs to discuss and draw the lines again in pen. Choose children to read aloud their pairs of matched words.

5 *WB page 150.* Talk about any two of the pictures, prompting the children to use *might* and *could* eg *It could be a box of chocolates. Or it might be a book. No, it's too big. It might be a bag etc.* The children then sit in their pairs to discuss what the presents might be and write the sentences. They then tell the class what they have decided.

Lesson Four

Aim	To revise parts of the body.
New language	None.
New words	*chin, bruise, black eye, absent*
Aids	Tape 19c.

Listening, reading and speaking
1 Revise the parts of the body by touching the appropriate parts as you name them. Teach *chin* in the same way.

2 **PB page 77** and **TAPE 19c.** Present and practise the dialogue in the usual way. Help the children work out the meanings of *absent, bruise* and *black eye*. Divide the class into two groups to read aloud the two parts before the children practise in their pairs.

3 Ask the class the questions at the bottom of the page.

Reading and writing
1 *WB page 151.* The children complete as much as they can of the picture crossword, then sit in their pairs to help each other. If they cannot complete the puzzle in their pairs, they sit in fours and then eights to find all the answers. If they are still stuck, they should ask you for help.

Lesson Five

Aim	To write a piece of continuous prose.
New language	None.
New words	None.
Aids	Tape 19c.

90

Reading

1 **PB page 77.** Play **TAPE 19c** while the children listen and follow in their books.

2 *WB page 152.* Choose a child to read aloud the instructions under the Word Box. Give the children ten or even fifteen minutes to read through the Unit to find and write all thirty words. They then sit in their pairs to compare and add to their lists. Check for understanding by asking children to read aloud their lists, translating as they do so.

Reading and writing

1 *WB page 153.* The children read the description at the top of the page silently, asking for help with anything they do not understand. Read aloud the instructions for writing a description of a person, and compare these with the description of Uncle Jim. Help the class write a description of somebody known to all of them, perhaps the school principal or a television character. Follow the suggestions on *WB page 153.* Give the children a few minutes to think about who they are going to describe and make up their first paragraph. Ask one or two children to tell you what they are going to write.

2 The children then write their descriptions. Walk around helping and checking their work. They should complete the exercise for homework. Remind the children to learn the spellings in the Word Box on *WB page 152* for a test next lesson.

UNIT TWENTY

Lesson One

Aim	Revision.
New language	None.
New words	*guard, news stand*
Aids	None.

Listening, speaking and reading
1 *WB page 153.* The children sit in their pairs to read each other's descriptions and check them for mistakes. Walk around helping and checking. Choose some children to read their descriptions aloud, correcting them if necessary.

Listening, speaking and writing
1 Do the spelling test in the usual way.

2 **PB pages 78 and 79.** The two pictures are similar, but not the same. Discuss the pictures with the children and ask questions about them. Find one thing that is different, and prompt the children to say what the difference is, using a pair of sentences like those at the top of **PB page 79.** Have the children sit in their pairs to find the eight differences. Let some of the children say the differences, using pairs of sentences. Then they write the eight pairs of sentences in their notebooks, and read them aloud around the class.

3 *WB page 154.* Do the first half of the exercise orally before the children, working in their pairs, write, then read aloud, their answers.

Lesson Two

Aim	Revision.
New language	None.
New words	None.
Aids	None.

Reading and writing
1 *WB page 155.* Read the description of Jack with the children, checking their understanding of the vocabulary by asking questions. Teach and explain the word *adjective* and ask the children to name adjectives for you to write on the board. Go through the description of Jack again, helping the children to pick out and underline all the adjectives.

92

2 Go through the description again orally, helping the children to say the opposite of all the adjectives eg *Jack is old and unhealthy. He is short and fat and weak.* The children then sit in their pairs to help each other write a new description, using the opposites of all the adjectives underlined. They should ask for help if they are not sure about anything. When they finish, they could draw a picture in their notebooks or on a piece of paper to illustrate their description. While they are working, walk around marking their work and helping where necessary.

3 **WB page 155**, Section Two. The children complete the exercise – either in class or for homework. Encourage them to use dictionaries to look up any words they are unsure of.

4 **WB page 156**, Section One. Working in their pairs, the children read the descriptions and write the names above each picture, then complete the exercise at the bottom of the page. At the end of the lesson, ask the class *Who's the first/second/third boy?*

Lesson Three

Aim	Revision.
New language	None.
New words	None.
Aids	Tape 20a.

Listening, reading and speaking
1 **PB page 80** and **TAPE 20a.** Present and practise the dialogue in the usual way. Divide the class into three groups to read the three parts aloud. Ask the class the questions at the bottom of the page.

Speaking and writing
1 **WB page 156.** This is the next part of the story from **PB page 80.** Read through the 'improved' first section and the simple middle section, then prompt the children to suggest how to make the story more interesting using adjectives. Let the children work in their pairs or groups of four to write their improved versions of the middle of the story and the end of the story in their notebooks. Let as many groups as possible read out their ending to the story, then let the class discuss which was the best/silliest/shortest/longest/the most interesting/boring/exciting.

Lesson Four

Aim	Revision.
New language	None.
New words	None.
Aids	Tape 20b.

Listening and writing

1 Play **TAPE 20b** once. Tell the children to listen carefully and write down the six jobs they hear mentioned. Ask children to read aloud their lists. If nobody got all six, play the tape again.

2 Present and practise the dialogue on **PB page 81** and the tape in the usual way. Divide the class into groups to read aloud the seven parts, then have the children read the dialogues in their pairs. Use the same language to ask the children what they want to be, prompting them to give reasons.

Reading and writing

1 **WB page 157.** Choose children to read the two lists at the top of the page aloud. The children then match the jobs and the descriptions by drawing lines between them. They sit in their pairs to check their answers before reading them aloud around the class.

2 **WB page 157,** Jobs Bingo. The children write the names of any of the jobs at the top of the page on their bingo cards. Call out the job descriptions for the children to check off their cards. Remember to make a note of them in case there are any arguments. Play a second game, this time letting a child call out the descriptions while you make notes.

Reading and speaking

1 The children work in their pairs to read through Unit Twelve in their Pupil's Books, asking for help with anything they are not sure about.

Lesson Five

Aim	Practice Test.
New language	None.
New words	None.
Aids	Enough spinners for the class in groups of four.

Listening, reading and speaking

1 **WB pages 158 and 159.** The children play the game. They spin the spinner in turn to move around the board. When they land on a sentence square they spin the spinner again. They look at the table at the top of the page and complete the sentence with the word next to the number they have thrown. So, if they spin a number one, they must use the word 'terrific' in the sentence; if they spin a number two, they must use the word 'bad' in the sentence, and so on. If the word is a good word (terrific, great, good), they move forward another three squares. If the word is a bad word (bad, terrible, awful), they move back three squares.

94

Reading and writing

1   The children open **WB page 160**. Explain that they are going to do a short test and that there should be no talking. Go through the instructions for question one and make sure the children understand what they have to do. When they have completed question one, do the same for the rest of the Test, question by question. The children then read through and try to improve their work. Collect in the books for marking. Points for marking: 1: 6; 2: 5; 3: 15 (one point for every correct adjective; one extra point for each sentence if the adjectives are in the correct order); 4: 5; 5: 10; 6: 9. Total 50 points.

TEST 5 (Units 17 – 20)

1 Draw lines to the words that mean the opposite.

square	unlucky
complicated	early
lucky	easy
curly	straight
late	plain
patterned	boring
rude	round
interesting	polite

2 Make sentences by putting the words in the correct order.

1 lost beautiful woollen he new sweater a thick blue

2 cat brown young striped she has little a

3 they car new have black big

4 spotted new T-shirt nice a have I black and white

3 What do they do?

Example: I'm a builder. I build houses.

1 I'm a mechanic. _____ .

2 I'm a librarian. _____ .

3 I'm a reporter. _____ .

4 I'm a tailor. _____ .

5 I'm a waiter. _____ .

6 I'm a clown. _____ .

7 I'm a dentist. _____ .

8 I'm a farmer. _____ .

4 Fill in the blanks.

Example: I ___went___ to the cinema last night.
      (go)

1 We _____ in a nice hotel on our holiday.
      (sleep)

2 My mother _____ a letter to the shop to complain about
          (write)

   the dress she _____ .
              (buy)

3 She _____ her new dress to the party.
        (wear)

4 She _____ so thirsty that she _____ six cups of tea.
        (is)   (drink)

5 Tom played his guitar while Susie _____ .
                                        (sing)

5 Write a passage of at least 75 words about either your favourite book or your favourite film. Make sure you tell:

When you read/saw it. What it's about. Why you like it.

6 Draw lines.

unwrap	door
unlock	package
unfold	shirt
unroll	suitcase
untie	poster
unpack	string
unscrew	bottle

97

7 **Draw lines to the words that mean the same.**

dangerous	unpatterned
simple	unsafe
sick	uninteresting
sad	unhappy
boring	unwell
plain	uncomplicated
single	unmarried

8 **Which word is different? Circle the different words.**

tastes	mixes	smells	sounds
plain	check	striped	spotted
thick	thin	large	beautiful
beefburger	lunch	sandwich	biscuit
didn't	can't	should	haven't
tractor	lorry	car	sleigh
pancake	pie	omelette	recipe

UNIT TWENTY-ONE

Lesson One

Aim	Revision.
New language	None.
New words	None.
Aids	Tape 21a.

Reading and speaking
1 Go through the marked tests in the Workbooks, helping children to understand any mistakes they made, and practising anything which has caused difficulties.

Listening, reading and speaking
1 Play **TAPE 21a** and read the dialogue on **PB pages 82 and 83** in the usual way. Discuss the questions at the bottom of **PB page 83**.

2 Ask questions about the conversation like this: *Who said they could bake a cake? Who said they would bring some lemonade?* etc. Draw children's attention to the change from *can to could*, and from *will to would* in reported speech. Practise orally in class saying sentences such as: *I can swim . . . I'll open the door. What did I say?* Prompt the response *You said you could swim . . . would open the door.*

3 Children can act the dialogue when they are familiar with the text.

Reading and writing
1 *WB page 162*. The children complete the exercise, using the Pupil's Book to help them. They sit in their pairs to compare their answers before reading them aloud around the class.

Lesson Two

Aim	To learn more about reported speech.
New language	*He said he was going home.*
New words	*peeling, mending*
Aids	None.

99

Reading and writing

1 Quickly revise the Present Continuous tense by giving individuals and pairs commands eg *Draw a house on the board/Write the numbers from one to twenty.* While they are doing it ask them *What are you doing?* and the class *What is she doing/What are they doing?*

2 *WB page 161.* Teach the new words using the pictures and write them on the board for the children to read and spell. Do the exercise orally before the children write the answers, check them in their pairs and then read them aloud around the class.

Listening, speaking and writing

1 Call a boy to the front. Say *(Name) is a very, very old man. He cannot hear well.* Ask a child to read out his answer to the first question on **WB page 163** and prompt the child at the front to mime not being able to hear and to ask you *What did he say?* Respond *He said he was looking for his glasses.* Repeat for all the other answers on **WB page 163.** Repeat twice with different children to ask and answer the questions.

2 *WB page 164.* The children complete the speech bubbles, then sit in their pairs to compare and check each other's answers before they read them aloud.

3 The children work in groups of three to act and practise the dialogue at the bottom of the page. Choose one group to demonstrate before they begin. Walk around helping and checking, and telling the children to change parts. At the end of the lesson, try to let all the groups demonstrate one of their dialogues.

Lesson Three

Aim	To use *asked, answered, replied* in reported speech.
New language	None.
New words	*President, reply, replied*
Aids	Tape 21b.

Listening, speaking and reading

1 Play **TAPE 21b**, stopping the tape after each question and prompting the class to try to answer it. Play the tape again straight through and ask the class to tell you what is happening. The children will probably know *President*. Then play the tape with **PB page 84** in the usual way. Divide the class into eight groups to read the eight parts.

2 Use the questions at the bottom of **PB page 84** as a way of introducing the new language. Extend the practice by asking similar questions about other people on the tape. Write some of their answers on the board for the class to read aloud.

Reading and writing

1 *WB page 165.* The children read the text silently, then choose children to read it aloud. Choose three good readers. Two read the two parts and the other

100

is the narrator and reads *said (or asked) Karen/said Jane*. This will make the dialogue sound really boring. Read aloud the instructions at the top of the page and make sure the children understand what to do.

2 Do the exercise orally, discussing the changes made. Write some of the suggested changes on the board for the children to read aloud. The children then work in their pairs to rewrite the dialogue using *answered, replied, asked and said*. Walk around helping and checking. Choose children to read aloud their dialogues at the end of the lesson.

Lesson Four

Aim	The children learn reported speech questions.
New language	*I asked if/whether the hotel was finished.*
New words	*whether, yet, reservations, finally*
Aids	None.

Listening, reading and speaking
1 **PB page 85.** Read through the newspaper article with the children, prompting them to guess the meaning of the new words and writing them on the board for the children to practise reading aloud. Read through the complete article, then have the children read it silently, asking for help if necessary. Help the class to complete the questions at the bottom of the page, and write them on the board for the children to read aloud. Leave sufficient space to write the answers later.

2 Ask the class the questions, and prompt them to find and say Mr Shark's answers eg

Reporter *Is the hotel very expensive?*
Mr Shark *It's a bit expensive, but not too expensive.*

Writing
1 **PB page 85.** The children work in their pairs to write out the questions and answers as above. Walk around helping and checking. Choose children to read their answers aloud and write them in the spaces on the board so the children can check and correct their work.

2 *WB page 166* takes the story a stage further with Mr Shark being questioned by a policewoman. Read through it first to check for understanding, then have the children transfer it to the report form underneath, using *asked if/asked whether*. Do about half of it as a class exercise before the children write, then read aloud, their answers.

Reading and writing
1 The first exercise on *WB page 167* is to help the children improve their dictionary skills. They should first work in pairs and put the ten words into alphabetical order. Check that they have done this correctly by getting children to read out their words in order around the class. They then look up the words in their dictionaries to check the meaning.

101

Lesson Five

Aim	A listening comprehension.
New language	None.
New words	*Braille, invented, code, domino, die*
Aids	Tape 21c. A domino.

Listening and speaking

1 Play **TAPE 21c** while the children just listen and then tell you what they have understood. Play the tape again, prompting the children to work out the meaning of the new words. Show them the domino and talk about the pattern of dots. Talk about codes – some of them may know about Morse or Semaphore. Look at **WB page 167** to see the Braille alphabet. If you are able to borrow some writing in Braille, it would be very interesting for the children to feel it. Play the tape again all through, then tell the children that they are going to have a listening test. Play the tape again.

Writing

1 **WB page 167.** Read aloud the sentences in number one, and prompt the children to say if they are true or false. The children then work in their pairs to write the other answers in their notebooks. Give them a last chance to listen to the tape again, then choose children to read aloud their answers.

2 **WB page 168.** The children work out the Braille message, and write it down.

3 Finish the lesson with the spelling test as usual.

Reading and writing

1 **WB page 169**. Introduce the new vocabulary to the children in the usual way. You could demonstrate the meaning of *translate* by translating a sentence of the reading task into the children's own language.

2 The children read the text silently as you move around the class, helping where necessary. Then, working in pairs, they answer the questions, writing *True or False*. Check these answers orally around the class.

3 The children then go on, in pairs, to list the words in their language that are difficult to translate into English. Ask them to suggest these words and write them on the board with their English translation. Finally they list the words in English that are difficult to translate into their own language. Ask for these and write them on the board with the translations. This section could be set for homework and checked at the start of the next lesson.

102

UNIT TWENTY-TWO

Lesson One

Aim	More practice with reported speech.
New language	Reported questions with *Wh* words.
New words	*team, lobster*
Aids	Tape 22a.

Listening, speaking and reading

1   Play, present and practise the dialogue on **PB pages 86 and 87** and **TAPE 22a** in the usual way.

2   *WB page 170.* Do this as a class exercise orally. Point out to the children that if the question does not begin with a *Wh* word, there must be an *if* or *whether* in the reported speech question. Do not labour this at this time. Ask the children to say the reported speech questions and write them on the board for the children to read aloud and copy into their Workbooks. The children should read through the exercise, looking for the difference between questions which begin with a *Wh* word and those which do not, and underlining the question words.

3   Divide the class into groups of three. They use **WB page 170** to practise dialogues like this:

> **Child 1**   *Do you like your job?*
> **Child 2**   *I can't hear. What did she say?*
> **Child 3**   *She asked Terry if he liked his job.*

When they finish, the children should change parts and repeat, then change parts again until all the children have read all the parts.

Lesson Two

Aim	More reported speech.
New language	None.
New words	None.
Aids	Tape 22b.

Listening, reading and speaking

1   **PB page 88** and **TAPE 22b.** Use these to present and practise the dialogue in the usual way. Divide the class into two to read aloud the two parts before the children practise reading in their pairs.

2   Choose children to read aloud and answer the questions at the bottom of the page.

Reading and writing

1 **WB page 171.** Give the children a few minutes to read the dialogue at the top of the page, then choose two children to read it aloud. Go through the exercise orally before the children write their answers, then sit in their pairs to check them before reading them aloud around the class.

2 Finish the lesson with the jumbled words exercises at the bottom of **WB page 171.** Encourage the children to use their dictionaries to check the meaning of any words they are unsure of.

Lesson Three

Aim	Revision of prepositions of motion.
New language	None.
New words	None.
Aids	None.

Listening and speaking

1 Revise *into, on, out of, towards, along, off, across* using demonstration and classroom objects.

2 Extend the revision by talking about the picture on **WB page 172** and prompting the children to make sentences about it.

Reading and writing

1 Write all the prepositions of motion on the board for the children to practise reading aloud.

2 The children write sentences about the picture on **WB page 172** using these words. They sit in their pairs to compare and check each other's answers before they read them aloud.

3 Ask the children *What's the woman with the basket doing?* and *What's the cat doing?* to prompt the responses *She's walking across the road. It's walking along the wall.* Write the questions on the board for the children to read aloud. Ask the children to write some more questions about the picture in their notebooks. Let them read aloud their questions, then have the children sit in their pairs to practise asking and answering the questions.

Listening

1 Play a game of Simon Says using the prepositions. Give commands like this: *Put your books into your bags. Take a book out of your desk. Push the book along your desk. Take the book off your desk. Point towards the door. Take your left foot out of your shoe. Put your right arm across your face etc.*

Reading and drawing

1 **WB page 173.** Choose children to read aloud the sentences at the top of the page. Explain to the children that their drawings must make clear what the person

104

is doing eg if they draw a man going into the post office, they should draw his back, not his front. When the drawings are completed, the children sit in their pairs to ask each other questions about their pictures.

Lesson Four

Aim	Consolidation of reported speech.
New language	None.
New words	*student, council, organise, meeting*
Aids	None.

Listening, speaking and reading
1   PB page 89. Read through the report with the children and help them to work out the meanings of the new words. If necessary, explain what a School Council is. The idea is that the children in a school elect representatives to meet with the teachers and the school principal to discuss school policy and problems and to help solve any problems. Finally, read through the whole report. The children then read it silently, asking for help with anything they do not understand or are not sure about. Choose children to read aloud and answer the questions at the bottom of the page.

Writing
1   *WB pages 174 and 175.* This is the meeting which was described in the report. Fill in the speech bubbles in the first two pictures as a class exercise, then let the children complete the work in their pairs, asking for help if necessary. Explain that if one person spoke more than once, the children should write what they said first in the top bubble; what they said second in the bubble below it, etc. Towards the end of the lesson, let the pairs join into fours to compare and check each other's work before they read aloud their dialogues.

Lesson Five

Aim	Listening practice.
New language	None.
New words	None.
Aids	Tape 22c.

Listening and writing
1   Practise the sound of *s* and *z*, first at the beginning of words (Sue, zoo) and then in the middle of words (police, please, this, these, eyes, ice) etc. Say words at random and prompt the children to say whether the sound is *s* or *z*. When they can do this fairly competently, say pairs of words (eg this/this, this/these) and prompt the children to say if they are the same or different.

105

2 *WB page 176.* Read aloud the instructions and make sure the children know what to do. Play the first ten pairs of words on **TAPE 22c** while the children just listen, then repeat while they tick the correct box. Choose children to read aloud their answers. Write the pairs of words on the board and play the tape again, this time saying *same* or *different* after each pair.

3 Repeat the whole process with the second list of pairs of words. You can find examples in the Tapescript for **TAPE 22c** at the back of the book.

Writing and speaking

1 *WB page 177.* This speaking task is designed to give the children practice in speaking without elaborate prompts. Stress to them that in this instance the ability to speak is as important as speaking absolutely correctly.

2 Give the children five minutes to make notes about their last holiday. Emphasise that they should not write sentences, just short notes and words to remind them of what they are going to talk about. As they are working, make notes about your own last holiday.

To give the children confidence, show them your notes and then talk very briefly about your last holiday. The children then sit in their pairs and tell each other about their holidays. Walk around noting any common mistakes. Do not correct the children now, revise the points in later lessons. The children then change partners and tell each other about their holidays.

3 Finish the lesson with the spelling test in the usual way.

UNIT TWENTY-THREE

Lesson One

Aim	Revision for the end-of-year test.
New language	None.
New words	None.
Aids	Tape 23a.

Reading and speaking
1   PB page 90. This revises the Present Simple and Continuous tenses and occupations. Look at the first three pictures and choose children to read the speech bubbles aloud. Ask the questions under each picture and prompt the children to answer. The children make up speech bubbles and questions for the other three pictures, then sit in their pairs to practise asking and answering the questions. If you can find suitable pictures of other occupations, extend the practice.

Writing
1   *WB page 178,* Section One. Revise *like, love, hate* using the pictures at the top of the page, then do the exercise orally before the children write their answers and read them aloud around the class.

2   *WB page 178,* Section Two. The children complete the sentences in pencil, then sit in their pairs to compare their work. They should ask for help if they cannot agree. They then read their completed sentences aloud. Give them time to correct any mistakes.

Listening, reading and speaking
1   Play the dialogues on **TAPE 23a** and **PB page 91** one by one and treat in the usual way. The children practise the dialogues and make up new dialogues in their pairs.

Lesson Two

Aim	Revision.
New language	None.
New words	None.
Aids	Tape 7a.

107

Listening, speaking and writing

1 **WB page 179.** Discuss the chart before the children fill in the spaces, then read aloud around the class. They then add more adjectives of their own choice and finish the chart, again reading aloud around the class.

2 **PB pages 26 and 27.** Play **TAPE 7a** while the children listen and follow in their books. **WB page 180.** The children match words in the two lists to make sensible sentences, then they sit in their pairs to compare and check their answers before they read them aloud. The children then work in their pairs to complete the sentences in the next exercise. Set the Word Snake puzzle for homework.

3 **WB page 181.** Give the children time to look at the two pictures, then prompt them to say what is different in the second picture eg *The small girl has bought a handbag. The girl with the spotted dress has bought a scarf, etc.*

Reading

1 Working in their pairs, the children read through Units Six to Ten, asking for help with anything they are not sure about.

Lesson Three

Aim	Revision.
New language	None.
New word	*spy*
Aids	Tape 23b.

Reading, writing and listening

1 **WB page 180.** Orally in class go through the answers to the Word Worm puzzle which the children did for homework. The following words could be found: *English, shout, out, door, doors, outdoors, safe, feed, dish, shop, shopping, in, giraffe, centimetre, time, metre, tree, trees, sugar, arm, chair, armchair.*

2 Have the children look at the dialogue on **PB page 92** and read it through quickly. Help them guess the meaning of *spy.* They then work in their pairs to write the questions in their notebooks and fill in the missing words. When they have finished, play **TAPE 23b** twice so they can correct their work. They then sit in their pairs, with the Pupil's Books and notebooks open, to practise the dialogue.

Speaking and writing

1 **WB page 182.** Do the first two exercises orally before the children write, then read aloud, their sentences. There are several possible answers for each question.

2 **PB page 48.** Give the children time to read the page silently, then choose children to read aloud the words in each picture.

3 **WB page 182,** Section Three. The children work in their pairs to write, then read aloud their answers.

108

Reading

1 Working in their pairs, the children read through Units Eleven to Fifteen, asking for help with anything they are not sure about.

Lesson Four

Aim	Revision.
New language	None.
New words	None.
Aids	Tape 23c.

Listening, reading and speaking

1 Play, present and practise the dialogue on **PB page 93** and **TAPE 23c** in the usual way. Move on to the second picture of the next week when the Field family were properly prepared for their guests. Ask questions about the first picture eg *What was Mrs Field doing when Mr and Mrs Booth arrived?* Accept short answers eg *She was in the bath. She was washing her hair.* The children can practise asking and answering similar questions in their pairs.

Reading and writing

1 *WB page 183.* Do examples of the first two exercises orally before the children work in their pairs to complete the lists, then read them aloud around the class.

2 Working in pairs, the children read through Units Sixteen to Twenty in their Pupil's Books, asking for help with anything they are not sure about.

Lesson Five

Aim	Revision.
New language	None.
New words	None.
Aids	None.

Reading and speaking

1 *WB pages 174 and 175.* The children read through the conversation, then read the report of the meeting on **PB page 89.**

2 Choose two children to read the two parts in picture one in the Workbook, then you read aloud the first paragraph of the report in the Pupil's Book. Choose another three children to read aloud the second and third pictures, then you read aloud paragraph two. Two children read aloud the last two pictures, then you read the last paragraph of the report.

3 *WB page 183,* Section Three. Go through each sentence in detail before the children write, then read aloud their answers.

Reading and writing

1 **WB pages 184 and 185.** Read aloud the story on **WB page 184,** telling the children they must try to work out the meanings of any new words by themselves. They read the story aloud around the class, sentence by sentence, just once, then read the story silently by themselves. The children then answer the questions on **WB page 185,** by themselves, in pencil.

2 When they have finished, or done as much as they can, begin to discuss their answers, praising correct ones and at the same time asking why they chose them. Help children who chose the wrong answer to see why it is wrong and point them towards the correct answer by using clues in the story.

3 The children, working in their pairs, read through Units Twenty-One and Twenty-Two, asking for help with anything they are not sure about.

UNIT TWENTY-FOUR

Lesson One

Aim	Revision.
New language	None.
New words	None.
Aids	**Tape 12b.**

Reading, listening and speaking
1 The children look at **PB page 49** and listen to Tape 12b. Write a list of the places from **WB page 92-3** on the board and ask the children to tell you what they go to each place for.

Reading and writing
1 Children turn to **WB page 186**, Section One. Go through the first three examples orally in class and then children work individually to match phrases. They can then check their answer in their pairs.

2 Children do the second exercise on **WB page 186** in their pairs. Remind them to use the past tense when describing last week's weather: It <u>was</u> sunny, It rain<u>ed</u>, etc.

3 Encourage the children to use their dictionaries to help them complete the first exercise on **WB page 187**. They can work in pairs. When they have finished, check their answers orally round the class.

4 Finish the lesson with a spelling test in the usual way.

Lesson Two

Aim	Revision
New language	None.
New words	None.
Aids	None.

Listening and speaking
1 In the class, walk towards the door saying I'm going to open the door. Then as you open the door, say I'm opening the door. Finally, point at the opened door and say I have opened the door. Do this with other classroom actions. Choose children to come out to the front of the class and demonstrate the actions while you say He's going to close the book. He's closing the book. He has closed the book.

111

Reading and writing

1   Children turn to **WB page 188** and do the exercise in their pairs. Check their answers by choosing children to read their sentences aloud.

2   Give the children a few minutes to look at the reading passage on **WB page 189** and read it silently. Encourage them to try and work out or guess the meaning of any words they are not sure of. Read the passage to the whole class. Ask the children to put up their hands to stop you if there is anything which they do not understand. See if other children in the class can explain. Let children work individually to try and answer the questions at the bottom of the page. They then work in their pairs to check their answers. Finally, go through the answers orally in the class.

Lesson Three

Aim	Test A.
New language	None.
New words	None.
Aids	Tape 24a.

Listening and writing

1   The children open their **Workbooks** at **page 184** and the **Pupil's Books** at **page 94**.

Explain that they are now going to do their first test and there should be no talking. Go through the instructions for Section One, then let the children underline the correct words. Repeat for all the other sections in Test A. You will need to use **TAPE 24a** for Section Seven. The children then read through and try to improve their work. Collect in the books for marking at the end of the lesson.

Lesson Four

Aim	The children do Test B.
New language	None.
New words	None.
Aids	Tape 24b.

Listening and writing

1   The children open at **WB page 192** and **PB page 96**. This time go through all the instructions with the children before they begin to write. For section eight, use **TAPE 24b**. Collect the books in for marking at the end of the lesson.

112

Lesson Five

Aim	Discussion of test.
New language	None.
New words	None.
Aids	None.

Reading and speaking

This lesson is devoted to looking through the marked Workbook tests, helping the children to understand any mistakes they made, and practising anything which has caused difficulties.

TEST 6 (Units 21 – 24)

1   Change the tenses.

Example: He said he was bored. 'I am bored.'

1   She replied that she hated watching football on television.

_____

2   She asked if we were going to Sarah's party.

_____

3   He answered that they came to school by bus.

_____

4   They asked us who our favourite pop singers were.

_____

5   He said that it was raining.

_____

2   Circle the correct word or words.

1   You use an iron to iron/ironed clothes.
2   She prefers riding/rode her bicycle to school.
3   I like to draw/drew pictures.
4   They're trying to go/going to the cinema tonight.
5   He wants to see/seeing the television programme on England.

3   Change these sentences.

Example: 'Are you too hot?' She asked if I was too hot.

1   'I don't like Tony.'

He _____ .

2   'We're going to go to Switzerland to ski.'

She _____ .

3   'How tall are you?'

He _____ .

114

4 Fill in the blanks. Use: | so   because |

1 I love Nadia _____ she's so kind.

2 I was very thirsty _____ I drank three bottles of cola.

3 She wants to be a reporter _____ she writes so well.

4 The dress was too expensive _____ I didn't buy it.

5 Fill in the blanks. Use: | before   after   when   while |

1 I do my homework _____ I go to bed.

2 We came back to Egypt _____ visiting England.

3 I watched television _____ my parents were out.

4 The baby cries _____ he is hungry.

6 What are the opposites of these words?

young _____   healthy _____   safe _____

start _____   closed _____   thin _____

strong _____   clean _____

7 The pilot of your plane is speaking

I'm sorry for the delay. But we should be taking off from the airport soon. So sit back and relax. I hope you are going to enjoy your flight. Our route this afternoon is going to take us over Malaysia. Our flight time to Hong Kong will be three hours.

What six things did the pilot say? Use 'He said'.

_____

_____

_____

_____

_____

What do you think he meant by these words?

route _____   flight time _____   delay _____

8 Read the passage and answer the questions. Write sentences.

Some people don't like to live in a house in the countryside. They say it's unsafe. They prefer to live in flats in cities. They say it's safe and you can usually find swimming pools, shops, cinemas and restaurants. People who live in houses in the countryside don't agree. They prefer the countryside because there you can have a nice garden with a barbecue and there aren't so many people around or so much noise or traffic.

1 Why do some people prefer to live in the countryside in houses?

_____

_____

2 Why do some people prefer to live in the city in flats?

_____

_____

UNIT TWENTY-FIVE

As the last week of term is always interrupted by various activities, just work through as much of the work below as possible, in any order you wish.

1   PB pages 98 and 99 – The Maze Game. The boy and girl want to go to the circus. The children must help them find their way through the maze by answering the questions in each circle and following the path that is the answer. If they make any mistakes, they will not get to the circus, and must go back to the beginning and try again.

2   *WB pages 194 and 195*. Look together at the eight pictures that tell the story. Discuss them fully with the children. Do they think it would be more interesting if they just wrote a sentence for each picture or if they added some descriptions? Will they use any direct speech? What adjectives could they use?

The children then work in pairs to write the story in their notebooks. Walk around the class helping, correcting and encouraging them if they get stuck. Let as many pairs as possible read out their stories.

3   *WB pages 196 and 197*. Do the giant Picture Crossword in class or in pairs.

4   *WB page 198*. Colouring by numbers. Children can do this task in class or for homework.

5   **Use **TAPE 25a to revise and practise the song on **PB page 100**.

6   **Do the two puzzles on ***WB page 199*. Give the children some help with the second puzzle by explaining that they can use each letter from the word *appointment* only once. Write up some sample words on the board: pen, tent, men.

7   *WB page 200*. The children read the letter, using the pictures as clues to help them work out what the missing words are. Let children read out their completed letters in class for you to check their answers.

8   PB page 101. The children find the hidden presents in the picture (toy plane, watch, gloves, book, cassette, shirt, ball, bicycle, chocolate, socks). Prompt the children to tell you where they are.

9   *WB page 201*. Children do the word snake puzzle. Use **TAPE 25b** to do the listening exercise in the usual way.

10   *WB page 202*. Find the twenty-five food and drink words in the wordsquare.

11   **Children draw a picture of their friend on ***WB page 203*. They can also write a description of their friend in their notebooks.

TAPESCRIPT

Tape 1a

Susie Hello, Nadia! How are you?
Nadia Hi! I'm fine, thanks, Susie. How are you?
Susie Fine. Look! The new Stevie Spellbound film is on. Would you like to go?
Nadia Oh, yes!
Susie How about this evening?
Nadia Sorry. I can't go this evening. I have to go to my piano lesson. Let's go tomorrow evening instead.
Susie I can't. My Mum's busy tomorrow. I have to look after my little brother.
Nadia Oh dear. Well, how about Sunday afternoon?
Susie Oh, I can't go then. I have to go and see my grandmother on Sunday. Let's go on Monday evening.
Nadia Oh, I can't. I have to go to my sister's house. How about Tuesday?
Susie Yes, Tuesday's fine.
Nadia OK. Tuesday.
Susie Oh no! We can't go on Tuesday!
Nadia Why not?
Susie Because the film ends on Monday!

Tape 1b

Boy 1 Hello! How are you today?
Boy 2 I'm fine, thanks. How are you?
Boy 1 I'm fine, too. Hey, I don't have any homework. Would you like to go to the cinema?
Boy 2 I'm sorry. No. I went to the cinema last week.
Boy 1 Oh dear. Well, how about a beefburger? Let's go for a beefburger.
Boy 2 No. I'm not hungry. But let's have a lemonade.
Boy 1 No! No, I can't. Cold drinks give me a toothache!
Boy 2 Well, how about the dentist? Go and see the dentist!
Boy 1 No, no . . . . .
Boy 2 Why not?
Boy 1 I have to do my homework. Bye!

Tape 1c

Narrator And now the results of the Montana Grand Prix.
First is Ben Harris! And only four seconds behind is Pete Johnson —
Pete Johnson is second.
And third is Nigel Brown!

Tape 1d

Narrator	1	chair	chair	6	pair	pair
	2	air	ear	7	your	year
	3	hear	hair	8	tear (v)	tear (n)
	4	near	near	9	stare	stare
	5	we're	wear	10	clear	Clare

Tape 1e

Reporter You drive a lot. Tell me . . . . . do you enjoy driving?
Mr al-Kuwari Oh, I LOVE driving. I love driving fast.
Reporter And . . . . . and . . . . . what about hobbies? What do you like doing?
Mr al-Kuwari Well — I love swimming. I like swimming in the sea, but really I prefer swimming in my beautiful pool.
Reporter Er . . . . .
Mr al-Kuwari And I love riding, especially on the beach.
Reporter Yes. Yes. Er . . . . . what about sports?
Mr al-Kuwari No. I HATE sports. I hate watching football and basketball. And I hate playing them, too.

Reporter	How about . . . . . reading?
Mr al-Kuwari	UGH! No. I HATE reading.
Reporter	Do you like going to the cinema or listening to music?
Mr al-Kuwari	Oh! I like going to the cinema and I love watching films about rally driving!

Tape 1f

Saeed	Hello. Karen? Mr al-Kuwari here. I'm at home. I've left my diary in the office.
Karen	Hello. Yes. It's here.
Saeed	I can't remember my appointments. What do I have to do next week?
Karen	Well, on Monday, that's the eighteenth, you have to go to Paris for the day.
Saeed	Yes. I remember that.
Karen	Then on the nineteenth you have to go to Madrid in the morning.
Saeed	OK. Madrid office. What about Wednesday?
Karen	The twentieth . . . . . um . . . . . you have to see the dentist in the morning, and you have to see Mr Foot in the afternoon.
Saeed	Right . . . . . dentist in the morning . . . . . . Mr Foot in the afternoon. What else?
Karen	On the twenty-first you have no appointments, but on the twenty-third you have to see Mr Hill at the bank in the morning . . . . . and you have to pick up Mr Brown from the airport in the afternoon.
Saeed	Mr Hill at the bank. Mr Brown at the airport. OK, Karen. Please put this appointment in my diary. I have to see Mr Lake on Thursday afternoon, at 2 o'clock.
Karen	Right, Mr al-Kuwari. Mr Lake . . . . . twenty-first . . . . . 2 o'clock.
Saeed	That's right. Thank you, Karen. See you tomorrow. Bye.
Karen	Goodbye.

Tape 2a

Peter	Hi, Andrew!
Andrew	Hi, Peter. How are you?
Peter	I'm fine. And you?
Andrew	Fine. Hey, I have a new job.
Peter	Great! Do you like it?
Andrew	Yes. It's really interesting. I travel all over the world, fly to lots of different places.
Peter	Really?
Andrew	I usually visit five or six different countries every week.
Peter	Yes?
Andrew	Yes. I work strange hours – and I work hard – but it's a great job.
Peter	Er . . . . . what IS your job?
Andrew	I'm a flight attendant.
Peter	But . . . . . but . . . . . your clothes. I don't understand.
Andrew	Oh! I'm not working today. I'm on holiday. I'm painting my son's bedroom today!
Peter	Oh. Now I understand. I thought it was your new job!
Andrew	Oh, no . . . . .

Tape 2b

Mrs Green	Clare – take off my shoes!
	Alan – get off the chair!
	Turn off the TV, please, Jane.
	Ben – put on your T-shirt.
	Look after Ben, Diane.
	Kate – get OUT of the cupboard!
	Now, everybody, let's get in the car. It's time to go out!

Tape 2c

Narrator	Good evening ladies and gentlemen. Welcome to the Brown Brothers' Circus! And here are the amazing Wonder Clowns!
	Well . . . . . look at them! Number 1 – he's the red clown – he's carrying a ball. Number 2 – the green and white clown – is ringing a bell. Look at Number 3 – wow, he's clever! He's all green. And he's riding a bicycle!
	Now . . . . . number 4, the blue and white clown, he's sitting on a chair.
	Number 5 is all blue – there he is – he's jumping through the circle.
	Where's number 6? Where's the little yellow clown? Oooh-oh, he's there! He's sleeping!
	OK, folks. That's all. Those are the amazing Wonder Clowns!
	And now . . . . .

119

Tape 3a

Susie What's that?
Nadia It's the programme for the school trip next Saturday.
Susie Oh, great! Where are we going?
Nadia London. We're leaving school at 7.30 and we're travelling by bus.
Susie How long will it take?
Nadia Er . . . . . well, we're stopping for coffee at 9 o'clock, and arriving in London at 10 o'clock.
Susie Then what?
Nadia First we're going to Madame Tussaud's Waxworks, then we're visiting the Houses of Parliament. Then we're having lunch.
Susie Yes. What are we doing in the afternoon?
Nadia Then after lunch we're travelling by boat on the River Thames and going to the Tower of London.
Susie Great!
Nadia Oh, wow! It says we're seeing 'Evita' in the evening!
Susie Great!
Nadia Then we're coming back . . . . . arriving back at school at 12 o'clock.
Susie Then on Sunday morning, we're all sleeping!

Tape 3b

Girl 1 I'm going to a film.
Boy 2 I'm having lunch at the club.
Girl 2 I'm visiting my relatives.
Girl 3 I'm going to a concert.
Boy 2 I'm watching a football game.
Girl 4 I'm seeing a play.

Tape 3c

Mr Short Well, Susie . . . . . have you enjoyed your English classes?
Susie Oh, yes, Mr Short. I've had a great time in England.
Mr Short When are you going home?
Susie I'm flying back next week. But first I'm going to London for two days. I'm visiting my cousin. She's having a party. And she's taking me shopping.
Mr Short Well, have a good time.
Susie Thanks. I'm coming back to England next summer, too . . . . . so, see you next year, Mr Short.
Mr Short No . . . . . I'm starting a new job next month. I'm moving to a new school.
Susie Oh, well . . . . . good luck.
Mr Short Good luck to you, too, Susie. Bye.
Susie Goodbye.

Tape 4a

Boy 1 What are you doing tomorrow, Karim?
Karim I don't know. I might go to the beach. Would you like to come?
Boy 1 Well . . . . . the sea might be too cold.
Karim Yes . . . . . well, we could go to the swimming pool instead.
Boy 1 Yes – that's a good idea!

Boy 2 What are you doing tomorrow, Reda?
Reda I'm not sure. I might go to the cinema.
Boy 2 Oh . . . . . can I come with you?
Reda Yes. We could see the new Star Trek film.

Boy 3 What are you doing tomorrow, Paul?
Paul Well, I don't know. I might go to the football match.
Boy 3 Yes. I might go too.
Paul OK. Let's go together. Then we could go for a beefburger afterwards.
Boy 3 Yes.

Tim What are you doing tomorrow, Alex?
Alex I don't know, Tim.
Tim Well, we could go to the museum.
Alex Yes. I could ask my brother . . . . . he might come, too.

Boy 4   What are you doing tomorrow, Jack?
Jack   I'm going to the theatre with my family. What are you doing?
Boy 4   I'm not sure. We might go to visit my grandmother, or I might go and buy some records.

Tape 4b

A   She hasn't called me.
A   She isn't at school today.
A   He's late.
A   Those two girls look very similar.
A   Her letter hasn't arrived.
A   That restaurant looks good.
A   Let's go and see that film.
A   Why is the baby crying?
A   He doesn't look very happy.

B   Her phone could be broken.
B   She might be sick.
B   The bus might be late.

B   They could be sisters.
B   It might arrive later.
B   Yes, but it might be expensive.
B   It could be boring.
B   He could be hungry.
B   He might have a toothache.

Tape 4c

Tom   What are you doing?
Reda   I'm packing. I'm going to Germany tomorrow, to visit my cousin.
Tom   Why are you taking so many clothes?
Reda   Well . . . . . I'm taking three sweaters – it might be cold in Germany. It might snow!
Tom   Not in September!
Reda   Well . . . . . I'm taking my anorak and an umbrella – it might rain.
Tom   Yes. It could be very wet!
Reda   But I'm taking my swimming trunks and sunglasses and suntan lotion – it could be hot.
Tom   I don't think so. It isn't hot in Germany in September!
Reda   Well . . . . . my cousin and I might go swimming. So I have to take my swimming trunks. And I'm taking my football boots – I might play football with my cousin.
Tom   OK.
Reda   And I'm taking my camera, and some presents for my cousin, and some magazines to read at the airport.
Tom   That's a good idea. The plane could be late.
Reda   Yes.
Tom   But why are you taking medicine?
Reda   Well . . . . . German food could give me a stomachache. That could be a problem.
Tom   I don't think so. But – shutting your suitcase could be a problem!

Tape 4d

Man 1   Oh, what a terrible day!
Man 2   What's wrong?
Man 1   First . . . . . my alarm clock didn't work so I got up late.
Man 2   Then I had to look for my socks.
Man 1   Then I went to my garage . . . . . but a thief broke in last night and stole my car!
Man 2   Oh, no!
Man 1   Yes. The police saw the thief and ran after him . . . . . but he ran away.
Man 2   So, I took my wife's car . . . . . but it broke down.
Man 1   Oh, dear.
Man 2   So I came to work by bus . . . . . and the bus was very full. I had to stand up!
Man 1   Well, now I can sit down.
Man 2   Look out!
Man 1   What?
Man 2   Don't sit down on that chair. It's broken.
Man 1   Oh . . . . . thanks. Whew! I'm going to have a cigarette.
Man 2   You should give up smoking. It's bad for you.
Man 1   Oh, be quiet!

Tape 5a

Sarah   Hello! I'm Sarah Martin. I'm ten. I live in Australia. I have a brother, Adam, and a sister, Magda. They are both older than me. Magda is fourteen and Adam is twelve.
I have lots of hobbies – I like reading and swimming; and I enjoy playing basketball. I love riding a horse and watching show-jumping.

121

I hate cooking and cleaning and washing.
I go to Bridge Street School. I like English and history.
I love listening to music – pop music is my favourite. And I like playing the guitar and the piano, too.

Tape 5b

Girl 1   Hello! We're Class 3. Next week we're going to the airport.
Girl 2   Yes – we're visiting Heathrow airport, near London. It's the busiest airport in the world.
Girl 3   We're going on a plane and meeting the flight attendants.
Girl 4   We're watching Concorde arrive from New York. It's the fastest passenger plane in the world. It travels faster than sound.
Girl 5   I'm taking my camera!
Girl 6   We're going to the air traffic control tower.
Girl 7   We're having lunch in the airport restaurant.
Girl 8   In the afternoon an airport fireman is talking to us about his job.
Girl 9   And a baggage handler is telling us about his job. And we're meeting an engineer.
Girl 10   It's going to be a terrific day!

Tape 6a

Mary   Hello, John!
John   Oh, hello, Mary.
Mary   What are you doing?
John   I'm looking for some new jeans. These light blue ones are too big . . . . . the legs are too long.
Mary   How about these dark blue ones?
John   Yes. They're OK.

John   What are you buying?
Mary   I'm looking for a sweater.
John   How about this pink one?
Mary   Ugh . . . . . no. I hate pink. I like this red and white striped one.
John   Yes. It's very nice.

John   I have to buy a shirt, too.
Mary   How about this?
John   No, it's too small.
Mary   What size are you?
John   Medium. Hey, I like this green one. Oh, but it's £32 – it's too expensive.
Mary   Here. Try this.
John   Yes. That's good. I like that.
Mary   I have to get a dress for my cousin's party.
John   Well, what's wrong with that red one?
Mary   OK. Wait a minute.
Oh, no . . . the waist is too small. It's too tight. And the skirt is too short. Ugh. I hate buying dresses. I might wear jeans for my cousin's party.
John   Good idea. Look! You can wear this T-shirt.
Mary   Hey, yes! That's terrific!

Tape 6b

Principal   Alex Bell, I am cross with you.
Your behaviour is terrible.
You are lazy.
You are bad.
You waste time.
You arrive late every day.
You talk too much and disturb other pupils.
You show off and you boast and you fight with other boys.
You don't finish your school work.
You never do your homework.
Your English is awful and your maths is worse.
Your only good subject is art.
You are the worst pupil in the school!
Oh, dear, oh, dear!

122

Tape 6c

Simon What did he say?
Alex He said he was cross with me.
He said my behaviour was terrible.
He said I was lazy.
He said I was bad.
He said I wasted time.
He said I arrived late every day.
He said I talked too much and I disturbed other pupils.
He said I showed off, and boasted and fought with other boys.
He said I didn't finish my school work.
He said I never did my homework.
He said that my English was awful and my maths was worse.
He said that my only good subject was art.
He said I was the worst pupil in the school!
Simon Oh, dear!
Alex Yes . . . . . he said that, too!

Tape 6d

Mrs Lake It is terrible. Hundreds of lorries, cars and buses drive along New Street every day, and the noise is awful. The motorcycles are the worst. All the parents are very worried. Children play in the street and one day an accident might happen. The traffic travels very fast. The traffic makes New Street dirty, too. I hate living in New Street . . . . . and it is all because of the traffic.

Tape 6e

Interviewer Excuse me, sir.
Man Yes, What is it?
Interviewer Could I ask you a few questions?
Man What about?
Interviewer About your shopping.
Man OK. What do you want to know?
Interviewer Well . . . what have you bought?
Man Some trousers. Some dark brown and yellow trousers.
Interviewer Er, yes. And were they expensive?
Man Yes, quite expensive. They're spotted. They're rather nice.
Interviewer Er, yes.
Man For my daughter.
Interviewer Oh, I see!
Interviewer Excuse me, madam.
Woman Oh, good morning.
Interviewer I wonder . . . . . could you tell me what you've bought?
Woman Oh . . . . . well . . . . . I wanted to buy some trousers, some dark blue trousers, but I couldn't find any.
Interviewer So you bought nothing?
Woman No . . . . . I bought a skirt instead. A dark green skirt . . . . . just plain, you know, no pattern. It's rather nice.
Interviewer Good, good . . . . . and could you tell me . . . . . was it very expensive?
Woman Expensive? Well . . . . . no not really, no.
Interviewer Thank you, madam.
Woman Not at all.

Interviewer Excuse me, sir.
Man Yes?
Interviewer I wonder . . . . . could you tell me what you've bought?
Man Why?
Interviewer Well . . . . . I work for a radio programme and . . . . .
Man Oh, I see . . . . . well, yes, OK, then. I bought a shirt, a pink and white striped shirt.
Interviewer I see . . . . . very good, sir.
Man Yes . . . . . I nearly bought a spotted shirt . . . . . but I thought the striped one was better. It's very nice . . . . . rather expensive . . . . . not cheap . . . . . but very nice.
Interviewer Thank you, sir.

123

Interviewer	Excuse me, miss.
Young woman	Yes?
Interviewer	Could I ask you a few questions?
Young woman	OK. Sure. Go ahead.
Interviewer	Well . . . . . could you tell me . . . . . what have you just bought?
Young woman	Oh . . . . . I didn't buy anything. I just looked at some red trousers . . . . . they were very cheap . . . . . but I didn't buy anything.
Interviewer	Thank you.
Young woman	That's OK. Bye.

Tape 7a

Susie	Look . . . . . would you like to see my holiday snapshots?
Friend	Oh, yes.
Susie	Here. This is our hotel in Turkey.
Friend	Oh. I thought you went to Greece.
Susie	No. Greece was too expensive so we went to Turkey again. Here's the swimming pool.
Friend	Oh, that's great. Did you swim every day?
Susie	Yes, every day. Last year we went in the autumn and it was too cold to swim. But this time it was fine. Here's the restaurant.
Friend	Did you eat Turkish food?
Susie	Yes, Turkish food is very good. But my little sister doesn't like trying new kinds of food, so she ate English food. Here's the beach.
Friend	Oh . . . . . great. Did you go windsurfing?
Susie	No.
Friend	Why?
Susie	Because it was usually too windy. Here's my sister and me . . . . . on the beach.
Friend	Why are you sitting under an umbrella?
Susie	Because it was too hot in the sun. This is the town.
Friend	Oh, why is it so busy and dirty?
Susie	Because there are too many tourists! Here's our plane. It was late . . . . . we waited ten hours at the airport.
Friend	Oh, how boring!
Susie	Yes. And I had too much baggage so I had to pay some money at the airport.
Friend	Why did you have too much?
Susie	Because I brought you a present. Here you are!
Friend	Oh, wow! Thanks.

Tape 7b

A	So . . . . . Jim's married now.
B	Yes.
A	How did he meet his wife?
B	Well . . . . . it was very funny. He met her because his alarm clock didn't work.
A	What?!
B	Well, his alarm clock didn't work one morning, and he got up late.
A	Yes.
B	He got up late so he missed the train.
A	Yes.
B	He missed the train so he walked to work. Well, it began to rain, and he didn't have a hat or an umbrella so he went into a shop and bought a hat. Well, the shop didn't have the right size so he bought a very big hat.
A	Yes.
B	The hat was too big so he couldn't see the kerb.
A	Yes.
B	He couldn't see the kerb so he fell down and he broke his leg.
A	Oh, no!
B	So . . . . . the ambulance came and took him to the hospital.
A	Yes.
B	And in the hospital, he met a nurse named Karen. And now they're married!
A	Well, that's amazing!

Tape 7c

Alan Hello. I'm Alan. I live in England.
In England the weather is hot in June, July and August and cold in December, January and February.
In summer we go to the beach and swim. We go out on our bicycles and have picnics. In winter, it's cold and it snows. We go ice skating. Sometimes it snows on Christmas Day, and we have a 'white Christmas'. We build a snowman in the garden.

Ryan Hi! I'm Ryan. I live in Sydney, in Australia.
In Australia the weather's hot in December and cooler in June.
In June and July we go on holiday to Bali where it's really hot. We go swimming and surfing in December and January. On Christmas Day we have a barbecue on the beach.

Tape 7d

Ryan I have a big family. I have two brothers and one sister. One of my brothers is older than me. His name is Tim. My other brother Danny is younger than me. My sister is older than me, too. Her name is Helen.
My mother's name is Pam Brown and my father's name is Bob.
My brother Tim is married. His wife's name is Sheila. They have two daughters, Charlene and Wendy. My sister Helen is married, too. Her husband is called Terry. They haven't any daughters, just a son, Ross.
My dad's brother is called Tom. His wife is Sarah and my cousins are Peter and Lyn. My father's mother is called Sonia and her husband, my grandfather, is Jack.
My other grandmother is Alice. My grandfather is dead now.
His name was Joe.
My mother has a sister, my aunt Sally. She's married to uncle Pete. They have three children, my cousins Sue, Sam and Jane.
I like big families. Do you?

Tape 8a

Tom Which subject do you have after break, Reda?
Reda Maths.
Tom Ugh. I hate maths. It's so boring. I prefer history.
Reda Oh . . . . . you're crazy! History's more boring than maths. Maths is the most interesting subject.
Tom No. History's better than maths. So is English.
Reda But . . . . . maths is more useful. You need maths . . . . . for shopping and things.
Tom Yes, maybe you're right. But I don't like maths . . . . . it's too complicated. History and English are more fun.
Reda What's the most difficult subject?
Tom Er . . . . . science.
Reda Oh, no. Science is easy! It's easier than maths!
Tom I don't think so.
Reda Well . . . . . that's because you're not as clever as I am, Tom!
Tom Maybe not, but I like all the fun subjects!

Tape 8b

New CHAMP!
Now BIGGER!
Now BETTER!
With thicker, darker chocolate.
The bar with more punch!

MUESLI bar
  the new fruity snack!
Now with more dried fruit.
It's tastier! It's crunchier!
Now cheaper at 45 pence!

Be younger . . . . .
Be more beautiful . . . . .
Be more special . . . . .
  Floating on a CLOUD 9 soap
  smoother,
  softer,
  lighter than air.

Tape 8c

Shop assistant	Can I help you?
Boy	Yes. We want a bicycle!
Father	Yes. Do you have a bicycle for my son?
Shop assistant	Well . . . . . there's this one, the Comet. It's the newest and fastest bike.
Father	How much is it?
Boy	Oh, wow! It's great!
Shop assistant	It's £500, sir.
Father	Oh, that's much too expensive. Do you have anything cheaper?
Shop assistant	Well . . . . . there's the Raleigh. That's a bit cheaper . . . . . £305. Or the Escort . . . . . that's much cheaper . . . . . only £250.
Father	Yes, well . . . . is the Escort a good bicycle?
Shop assistant	It's a bit heavier than the Raleigh, and of course it's a lot slower than the Comet . . . . . but it's a very good bicycle, sir.
Boy	Oh, Dad. The Comet's a lot better.
Father	Yes, I know . . . . . but it's twice as expensive! OK . . . . . Can we have the Escort, please?
Boy	Can I ride it home?
Father	No . . . . . you must have some lessons first. You have to be much more careful before you can take this bike on the road.

Tape 9a

Peter	So . . . . . have you been to lots of interesting places?
Andrew	Yes. This job's fantastic! I visit so many places.
Peter	Have you ever been to Berlin?
Andrew	Yes. I've flown to Europe a lot. I've been to Berlin, Paris, Brussels, Rome, London, Lisbon, Oslo . . . . .
Peter	Really?
Andrew	Yes. I flew to Rome last Monday and Oslo last week. I flew to Paris and Brussels last month.
Peter	How about the Middle East? Have you ever been to Cairo? Or Sanaa? Or Damascus?
Andrew	Well . . . . . I've never been to Sanaa, but I've often been to Cairo and I went to Damascus last month.
Peter	Have you been to Hong Kong?
Andrew	Yes. I flew there in April. And I flew to Singapore, too.
Peter	Have you ever been to Japan?
Andrew	Yes. I flew to Tokyo in February, and I went to Seoul, too.
Peter	Wow! Seoul! I've never been there . . . . . or Japan . . . . .
Andrew	Well, maybe you should change your job!
Peter	Yes, maybe!

Tape 9b

Sarah	Hello again! I live in Australia. I've lived here for six years, since I was four. I go to Bridge Street School – I've been a pupil there for five years. I play the guitar. I started guitar lessons two years ago. And I started piano lessons six years ago, when we moved here. My best friend is Helen. She's been my best friend since I started going to school here. I also have a penfriend, Amina, in Pakistan. Amina has been my penfriend for two years. I have a new bicycle. My father bought it for me for my birthday three months ago.

Tape 10a

Teacher	Why are you late?
Pupil	Because of the bus.
Teacher	What happened?
Pupil	It broke down so I cycled to school.
Teacher	I see. Why were you absent yesterday?
Pupil	Because I was sick.
Teacher	I see. Where are your books? Why haven't you brought your books?
Pupil	My bag's broken so I can't carry my books.
Teacher	I see. Why are your shoes wet and dirty?
Pupil	Because my bicycle is broken so I fell in a puddle on my way to school.

126

Teacher	I see. Why are you yawning?
Pupil	Because I'm tired. My bed broke last night so I didn't sleep very well.
Teacher	I see. Your hair isn't very neat!
Pupil	Yes, well . . . . .
Teacher	I know, I know . . . . . your comb's broken so you can't comb your hair!
Pupil	Yes.
Teacher	I see. Well, go and stand at the back of the class.
Pupil	Can I sit down?
Teacher	No. The chair's broken so you have to stand up!

Tape 10b

Dad	Right. Let's go. Joe, have you packed the barbecue things?
Joe	Yes, Dad.
Dad	Sue, have you put the football things in the car?
Sue	Yes, Dad.
Dad	Margaret, have you locked the back door?
Mum	Yes, dear.
Dad	And have you closed the windows?
Mum	Yes, dear.
Dad	OK. Oh, Sue, have you locked all the windows and doors?
Sue	Yes, Dad.
Dad	OK. Oh, have you turned off the oven?
Mum	Yes, dear.
Dad	And turned off the television?
Joe/Sue	Yes, Dad!
Dad	Good. OK. Let's go . . . . . Oh, have you brought the camera?
Joe	Yes, Dad.
Sue	Oh, hurry up, Dad. It's almost lunchtime and we haven't started!
Dad	Right. Good. Yes. Let's go, then . . . . . Oh . . . . .
Mum	What is it?
Dad	I haven't put any petrol in the car.
Mum/Joe/ Sue	Oh, no!

Tape 10c

Oh, we can play on the big bass drum,
And this is the way we do it.
Boom, boom, boom goes the big bass drum,
And that's the way we do it.

Oh, we can play on the triangle,
And this is the way we do it.
Ting, ting, ting goes the triangle,
And that's the way we do it.

Oh, we can play on the piano,
And this is the way we do it.
Plink, plink, plonk goes the piano,
And that's the way we do it.

Oh, we can play on the violin,
And this is the way we do it.
Eee, eee, eee goes the violin,
And that's the way we do it.

Oh, we can play on the silver flute,
And this is the way we do it.
Toot, toot, toot goes the silver flute,
And that's the way we do it.

Tape 11a

Diane	Hi. What are you doing?
Mum	We're deciding where to go on holiday next summer.
Diane	Oh, great! I want to go to Malaysia.
Mum	Why Malaysia?
Diane	Because it's hot! I want to lie on the beach . . . . . I want to get a suntan. I want to be really lazy for two weeks!
Peter	Oh, no! That's really boring!
Mum	Well, what do you want to do, Peter?
Peter	Me? I want to do something more exciting. I want to go windsurfing or climbing or skiing or something. I don't want to lie around and do nothing!
Dad	What about you?

127

Mum	Well, I don't know . . . . . I want to see interesting places, you know, museums and art galleries. I want to look at monuments and things. And I want to go shopping, of course.
Diane	What do you want to do, Dad?
Dad	I want to relax, you know . . . . . I want to paint a bit, read a bit, drive through the countryside. I want to watch birds, swim a little, just relax.
Diane	So, ... like I said . . . . . Malaysia's just the right place for us!
Peter	For you, Diane!
Diane	No, for all of us. It has hot weather, good beaches, windsurfing, waterskiing, tennis, swimming, interesting places, monuments and things, nice countryside . . . . . it's just right.
Mum	Well, maybe you're right.
Diane	Yes . . . . . it's going to be great . . . . . And I want to eat different food, too!

Tape 11b

Sarah	I think it's important to be healthy so I like to keep fit. I like to get up early and do my exercises. I like to do situps and pushups and bending exercises. I think it's important to eat healthy food, too. So for breakfast I like to have fresh fruit and brown bread. I never eat sugar or meat, and I never drink tea or coffee – they are bad for you. I like to walk or cycle to work, and I like to swim in my lunch hour. In the evenings I sometimes play basketball or tennis. I like to play at least twice a week. I feel great!

Tape 11c

Sarah	I do a fifteen minute workout every morning.
Helen	Oh, I prefer to workout in the evening. I go to a Keep Fit class twice a week.
Sarah	Do you like it?
Helen	Yes, it's fun. I prefer to do my workout together with friends. It's more interesting.
Sarah	I swim with my friends . . . . . we like to go swimming during the lunch hour.
Helen	Oh, I prefer to go swimming on Sunday. It's more relaxing.
Sarah	And I like to play sports with my friends. We play basketball or tennis.
Helen	Yes. I like to play basketball, too. But I don't like tennis. I prefer to play volleyball! I play volleyball with my brother.
Sarah	Oh, does he like to keep fit?
Helen	My brother! No! He prefers to be lazy!

Tape 11d

Mary	Dad?
Dad	Yes.
Mary	At night, when it's dark, does the sun switch off?
Dad	No. The sun always shines. When our side of the Earth is near the sun, it is day. When the sun shines on the other side, it is night.
Mary	How big is the sun?
Dad	It's very big – over 1000 times larger than the Earth.
Mary	Wow! That's big! Which planet is nearest the sun?
Dad	Mercury.
Mary	How big is Mercury?
Dad	Oh, it's a small planet. It's about three times smaller than the Earth.
Mary	What's the next planet?
Dad	What? The next planet to the sun? Er . . . . . Venus. You know, you can see Venus just before the sun comes up or just after the sun goes down. It's called the 'morning star' or the 'evening star'.
Mary	So, Mercury is nearest to the sun, then Venus.
Dad	That's right.
Mary	So, what's next?
Dad	The Earth. The Earth is the third planet from the sun.
Mary	And the Earth goes around the sun?
Dad	Yes, that's right. The Earth travels around the sun. It takes one year. And the moon goes around the Earth. It takes one month.

Mary	How big is the moon?
Dad	Not very big – about a quarter the size of the Earth.
Mary	And the next planet is Mars?
Dad	Yes, that's right. Mars is about half as big as the Earth.
Mary	And then there's Saturn.
Dad	No . . . . . then Jupiter. Mercury, Venus, Earth, Mars, Jupiter. Jupiter is the biggest planet. Then Saturn. Saturn is the sixth planet from the sun.
Mary	I see. Mercury, Venus, Earth, Mars, Jupiter, Saturn.
Dad	That's right. Why are you asking me all these questions?
Mary	I'm doing my science homework.
Dad	No, you're not. I'm doing your science homework!

Tape 12a

Sammy	Hey! Where are you going?
Karim	I'm going into town.
Sammy	Oh yes? What for?
Karim	To visit the hardware shop.
Sammy	What for?
Karim	To buy some parts for my bicycle.
Sammy	Why?
Karim	To mend it. It's broken. OK?
Sammy	Oh, I see. Can you mend it?
Karim	I don't know. Mum is going to help me. I want to mend it today so I can ride it this afternoon.
Sammy	Why?
Karim	To go to the beach.
Sammy	Why?
Karim	To go swimming.
Sammy	Why?
Karim	Oh, be quiet, Sammy! Why do you ask so many stupid questions?
Sammy	To make you cross!

Tape 12b

Tina	What's a library?
Susie	You go to a library to borrow books.
Tina	Oh. And a cinema?
Susie	You go to a cinema to watch films.
Tina	I see. What's that?
Susie	It's a stadium. You go there to watch football games.
Tina	Right. And that?
Susie	That's a hospital. You go there to see a doctor when you're ill.
Tina	And that's a restaurant!
Susie	Yes. You go there to eat.
Tina	What's this? A post office?
Susie	Yes. A post office. You go there to buy stamps and to post letters.
Tina	And there's an ice cream shop . . . . . you go there to buy ice cream!
Susie	That's right.
Tina	Great. . . . . . Let's go there!
Susie	OK!

Tape 12c

I have six pence,
I have six pence,
I have six pence to last me all my life.
I have two pence to spend,
and two pence to lend,
and two pence to take home to my wife.

I have four pence,
I have four pence,
I have four pence to last me all my life.
I have two pence to spend,
and two pence to lend,
and nothing to take home to my wife.

I have two pence,
I have two pence,
I have two pence to last me all my life.
I have two pence to spend
and nothing to lend,
and nothing to take home to my wife.

I have nothing,
I have nothing,
I have nothing to last me all my life.
I have nothing to spend,
and nothing to lend,
and nothing to take home to my wife!

Tape 13a

Principal Good morning.
Father Good morning. I'm Mr Grey. This is my son, Tony.
Principal Oh, yes, Mr Grey. I remember. Tony would like to come to our school.
Tony Yes, that's right.
Principal OK. Well . . . . . let's just get the papers and forms filled in.
Principal Now . . . . . address . . . . . Where do you live?
Father Well, we're still living in London. We're moving to Oxford soon.
Principal I see. So . . . . . what's your new address in Oxford?
Tony 16 Park Road.
Principal OK And, when are you going to move here?
Tony Next month, the 23rd.
Principal Good. Now, Tony, what is your full name?
Tony Anthony John Grey.
Principal And how old are you?
Tony Twelve.
Principal Right. And what is your date of birth?
Tony August the nineteenth.
Principal Now, Tony . . . . . Which subjects did you study at your other school?
Tony Oh, maths, English, history, geography, science . . . . . uh . . . . . art.
Principal I see. Did you study French?
Tony No, I never learned French.
Principal OK. And what was your favourite subject?
Tony Oh, I liked English and history best.
Father Yes . . . . . he's very good at history.
Principal Fine. Now, what sports have you played, Tony?
Tony Football and basketball.
Principal All right. Have you ever played tennis?
Tony No.
Principal Oh. Well you can play tennis here.
Tony Great!
Principal OK. That's all. Sorry there were so many questions.
Father That's all right.
Principal So, Tony . . . . . see you next month. Come to the office when you arrive on your first day.
Tony Yes. Thank you. Goodbye.
Principal Goodbye.

Tape 13b

Faisal Hello.
Britta Hello. Where are you from?
Faisal Malaysia. I live in Penang.
Britta I'm Swedish. I'm from Stockholm.
Faisal Oh . . . . . that's a cold country!
Britta Yes. In winter it's very cold and there's a lot of snow.
Faisal How cold is it?
Britta Sometimes it's minus 20°C.
Faisal Oh!! I prefer warm weather. In Penang it's about 30°C. all year round.
Britta That sounds great!
Faisal Yes. We go swimming. Penang is an island so we have some great beaches.
Britta We go swimming in the summer. In the winter we go skiing.
Faisal What language do you speak?
Britta Swedish. What about you?
Faisal I speak Bahasa Malay.
Britta Oh . . . . . do you eat curry all the time?
Faisal Well . . . . . we eat hot, spicy foods, but we also eat a lot of fruit and rice. I don't eat pork because I'm a Muslim. What do Swedish people eat?
Britta Well, a lot of fish . . . . . and very good cakes . . . . . and we drink a lot of coffee.
Faisal Do you wear lots of clothes in winter?
Britta Yes . . . . . thick coats. And we wear hats and scarves and gloves and thick boots.
Faisal In Malaysia we don't need so many clothes. We wear light, cool clothes . . . . . and both men and women wear a skirt called a sarong.
Britta It sounds nice. Maybe I should visit Malaysia.
Faisal Yes. It's a good place for a holiday!

Tape 14a

Tom What was it like?
Karim Oh . . . . . fantastic!
Tom Isn't it the biggest marine park in America?
Karim Yes, that's right. It's 125 acres – and there are fifteen different shows!
Susie Wow! Doesn't it have a killer whale show?
Karim Yes – Shamu, the killer whale, gives a show in the stadium. The stadium's very big – 3000 people can watch the show and the pool where Shamu swims has one million gallons of water!
Tom Aren't there dolphins, too?
Karim Yes, that's right . . . . . and seals and otters.
Nadia Didn't you get bored . . . . . just watching seals and whales all day?
Karim Oh no. There's lots more . . . . . there's a waterski show, too. And a deer park and a Hawaiian park with canoes and waterfalls, and a Japanese park.
Susie It sounds great!
Karim Yes, it WAS great!
Susie Can't you feed the animals?
Karim Yes . . . . . you can feed the dolphins and seals and birds. And you can cross through a pool full of sharks . . . . .
Tom Weren't you scared?
Karim Oh no . . . . . you don't SWIM through the pool – you go through a glass tunnel!
Nadia Haven't you brought any snapshots?
Karim Yes . . . . . here they are. Look.

Tape 14b

Mother Oh, Alex!
Alex What?
Mother Why haven't you cleaned your room?
Alex Oh, well . . . . .
Mother And why haven't you put away your books? And why haven't you washed your clothes? And why haven't you made your bed?
Alex Well . . . . . I . . . . .
Mother Oh . . . . . and haven't you finished your homework?
Alex No . . . . . well . . . . .
Mother Oh . . . . . really, Alex!

Tape 14c

Hickety, pickety, my black hen,
She lays eggs for gentlemen.
Gentlemen come every day,
To see what my black hen does lay.
Sometimes nine and sometimes ten,
Hickety, pickety, my black hen.

There was a crooked man,
And he walked a crooked mile.
He found a crooked sixpence,
On a crooked stile.
He bought a crooked cat,
And it caught a crooked mouse,
And they all lived together,
In a little crooked house.

Tape 15a

1 Don't Eskimos live in a *cold* country?
2 Can't Alice speak *French*?
3 Doesn't *John* play football?
4 Isn't Tom your *cousin*?
5 Doesn't *Susan* have your book?
6 Don't you *cycle* to school?
7 Didn't he *post* the letter?
8 Haven't we *finished* this exercise?

Tape 15b

Woman Good morning, Miss Black.
Girl Good morning.
Woman Now . . . . . you're looking for a job here . . . . . yes?
Girl Yes.
Woman OK. When did you leave school?
Girl Last year . . . . . after I finished my exams.
Woman I see. Can you type?
Girl Yes. I learned to type while I was at school. I took a typing class in the evening.
Woman I see. All right. Now . . . . . what did you do last year?
Girl Well, after I left school I worked in a shop for a few weeks, and when the shop was closed, on Wednesdays, I studied French and German. I studied some French while I was at school, but I wasn't very good then . . . . . I'm much better now.
Woman Fine.
Girl And then I worked in a restaurant for a few months.
Woman Why did you leave the shop?
Girl Well . . . . . I got the job in the restaurant before I left school, but the job didn't start immediately. I had to wait until January so I worked in the shop while I waited.
Woman OK. Why did you leave the restaurant?
Girl Well . . . . . I left when the boss left. I didn't really like the new boss.
Woman I see. Well, I think you can have a job here, but you must take a typing test before you start. Come into the other office and I can give you the test.
Girl Thank you very much.

Tape 16a

Teacher Well . . . . . the cleaning lady says she heard the window break while she was cleaning the Principal's office . . . . . that was at about 2.15. Now, Reda, what were you doing at 2.15?
Reda I was doing science, in Mr Major's class.
Teacher And you, Karim? What were you doing?
Karim I was doing English, in Room 205.

Teacher	Right. What were you doing, Tom?
Tom	I was doing English, too.
Teacher	And Peter?
Peter	I was in the office, sir. I was giving the secretary a letter from my mother.
Teacher	And you, Walid?
Walid	I was sitting in the library, waiting for the maths class to start.
Teacher	What about you, Paul?
Paul	John and I were putting on our overalls . . . . . for the art class.
Teacher	And what were you doing, Alex?
Alex	Me? I was putting away the football, sir.
Teacher	Is that ALL you were doing?
Alex	Well, I was kicking it, too.
Teacher	And?
Alex	And . . . . . uh . . . . . and
Teacher	And you kicked it through the window?
Alex	Yes, sir.

Tape 16b

Mrs Johnson	Hello, Mike. It's Mum.
Mike	Hello, Mum.
Mrs Johnson	Happy birthday, dear.
Mike	What? Oh, yes . . . . . thanks . . . . . uh . . . . .
Mrs Johnson	Are you all right? You're not ill?
Mike	No, Mum. I'm just tired. I was sleeping.
Mrs Johnson	Sleeping? But it's 12 o'clock. I was having my lunch.
Mike	It's three o'clock in the afternoon here. We have a siesta and go back to work later.
Mrs Johnson	Oh, sorry, dear. Anyway, happy birthday!
Mike	Thanks, Mum. Bye.
Mrs Johnson	Hello, Alison.
Alison	Oh . . . . . uh . . . . . Hello – is that you, Mum?
Mrs Johnson	Yes, dear. Happy birthday.
Alison	What? Oh, yes . . . . . thank you, Mum.
Mrs Johnson	What are you doing, dear?
Alison	Well, Mum, I was sleeping!
Mrs Johnson	What? Oh, dear. What time is it there?
Alison	Uh . . . . . let me look . . . . . it's midnight!
Mrs Johnson	Oh, I'm sorry, dear. I just wanted to say 'happy birthday'.
Alison	Well, you're too late . . . . . my birthday was yesterday . . . . . it's midnight here . . . . . it's almost tomorrow! Thanks anyway, Mum. Goodbye.
Mrs Johnson	Goodbye.

Tape 16c

Why was Walter washing with warm water?
Where were William and Walter walking?

Tape 16d

1 ball	**2** fall	**3** far	**4** bar	**5** beat
6 feet	**7** bed	**8** fed	**9** fell	**10** bell

Tape 16e

1 Fred, bread
2 bridge, bridge
3 fat, bat
4 bill, fill
5 feed, feed

Tape 17a

Policewoman	Mrs Pool left her room at 10.20 and went to Reception. She returned to her room at 10.40 and her bracelet was gone.
Manager	Yes, that's right.
Policewoman	So . . . . . we know the thief took it at about 10.30.
Manager	Yes, yes. I guess so.
Policewoman	What were you doing at 10.30?
Manager	Me? I was talking to Mrs Pool in Reception. She was asking me about the bus to the airport.
Policewoman	I see. Now what about the other people who work in the hotel? How many people work here?
Manager	Well . . . . . let me think . . . . . the cook, maid, waiter, and my secretary.
Policewoman	What was the cook doing at 10.30?
Manager	She was in the kitchen, cooking dinner.
Policewoman	And the maid?
Manager	Uh . . . . . she was working, in Room 8, I think. My secretary was typing letters in the office.
Policewoman	And what was the waiter doing?
Manager	He was working in the restaurant.
Policewoman	I see. Thank you. Now, I would like to see the hotel guests. I have to ask them what they were doing last night.

Tape 17b

Man 1	I'm a dentist.
	I look after people's teeth.
Woman 1	I'm a doctor.
	I look after ill people.
Man 2	I'm a farmer.
	I look after my cows and I grow vegetables.
Man 3	I'm a mechanic.
	I mend broken cars.
Woman 2	I'm a reporter.
	I write for the newspaper.
Man 4	I'm a waiter.
	I bring food to people in a restaurant.
Man 5	I'm an actor.
	I act in the theatre or in films.
Woman 3	I'm a librarian.
	I lend books to people in the library.
Woman 4	I'm a painter.
	I paint pictures.
Man 6	I'm a painter, too.
	I paint houses.
Man 7	I'm a builder.
	I build houses.
Man 8	I'm a tailor.
	I make clothes.
Man 9	I'm a clown.
	I make people laugh.
Women 5/6	We're musicians.
	We play in a pop group.
Woman 5	I'm a singer.
Woman 6	And I'm a guitarist.

Tape 18a

Assistant	Hello. Can I help you?
Boy	I'm looking for a birthday present for my mother.
Assistant	I see. Do you want something useful?
Boy	I don't know.
Assistant	Well, there are these useful red striped cotton towels.
Boy	No . . . . . I don't think so . . . . .

Assistant	Well, how about a beautiful new pink striped scarf? Or there's this funny big chocolate rabbit. Or . . . . .
Boy	No, not really . . . . . I just want something small, and not too expensive.
Assistant	I see. Maybe some ear-rings?
Boy	Yes.
Assistant	Well, there are some nice big round ear-rings here – or some long, thin, bright silver ones.
Boy	Oh, the gold ones, please.
Assistant	Right. That's £20, please.
Boy	Oh, well . . . . .
Assistant	Or there are some cheaper small square bronze ones. £8.
Boy	Oh, yes, those, please.
Assistant	Here you are. £8, then. Thank you.
Boy	Thank you. Goodbye.

Tape 18b

Girl	What are you cooking?
Boy	A new recipe . . . . . Fruit and Peanut Pancakes.
Girl	Mmmm. That sounds interesting. What's in it?
Boy	Bananas, pineapple, oranges, peanuts.
Girl	Can I help?
Boy	Well, can you get the chocolate sauce from the refrigerator?
Girl	OK. Wow . . . . . this looks good!
Boy	Right. Now I have to cook the pineapple and peanuts for ten minutes, with some egg.
Girl	It smells great!
Boy	OK. All finished. Do you want some?
Girl	Yes!
Boy	Here you are. How is it?
Girl	Well . . . . .
Boy	Well what?
Girl	Well, it tastes awful!
Boy	Oh, no!

Tape 18c

Red leather, yellow leather, red leather, yellow leather . . . . .

She sells seashells by the sea shore.
The shells she sells are seashells, I'm sure.

Tape 18d

1	back	**3**	bend	**5**	vet	**7**	bet	**9**	vend
2	very	**4**	boat	**6**	visit	**8**	vote	**10**	berry

Tape 19a

Yesterday Mr David Cook, an unmarried teacher from Maine, began his journey around the world in a rowing boat. He said he was uncertain how long it would take because he was unsure about the wind.

His brother, Paul Cook said, 'It's a very unwise trip! I think David is crazy. The boat is unsafe and it's a long and dangerous journey.'
But David Cook said, 'I am not worried. I'm sure I'm going to make the trip, and finish it unhurt.'

Bob Wells, the pop star, has been ill for many months. Last night he gave his first concert since last April . . . . . and it was very unexciting! Wells looked unhealthy and unhappy. His hair was uncombed and his clothes were untidy. The music was uninteresting . . . . . it was most unlike the terrific Bob Wells concerts we heard last year!

For sale: A baby bed . . . . . in good order . . . . . unused . . . . . unbroken £50
    (208) 335-5684

Yesterday Sue Snow, the film star, said, 'I think the newspaper reporters are very unkind about me! The dress I wore to the Hollywood party was simple and unpatterned – but it was also VERY expensive! It was NOT a SACK, as one newspaper said!'

Tape 19b

Andrew What is it?
Penny I don't know.
Andrew Well.....untie the string.
Penny OK. OK.
Andrew Hurry up.....Now, unwrap it. What is it?
Penny It's a book.....and a poster.
Mum What is the picture? Go on.....unroll it.
Penny Wow! It's a Michael Jackson poster! Great! What's yours, Andrew?
Andrew I don't know yet.
Mum Well, unwrap the package.
Andrew It's a box.
Penny What's in it? Unpack it.
Andrew It's a train! And a.....what's this?
Mum Unfold it. Oh, it's a T-shirt. That's nice.
Penny There's a present here for you, Mum.
Mum Let's unwrap it. Oh, it's a bottle of perfume.
Penny What does it smell like?
Mum Let me unscrew it. Mmm, that's nice. Thank you, dear.
Penny OK. That's all. Thanks, Dad!
Mum Right, Andrew, would you unlock the back door, please, and take all this paper out to the rubbish bin. Then it's time for dinner.
Dad Dinner.....great! It's good to be home again.

Tape 19c

Teacher Where's Tina today? Is she absent?
Girl Yes, she's in hospital.
Teacher Why? What's the matter with her?
Girl Well.....she has a broken leg. Her brother Alex is in hospital, too. He has a broken arm, and a broken toe. His leg is badly hurt, but it's unbroken.
Teacher Oh, dear!
Girl And Tina cut her lip and her chin and broke two teeth!
Teacher Oh, no!
Girl Yes. And her brother hurt his nose and has a cut knee. And Tina has a black eye, and they both have bruises.
Teacher What happened? Were they fighting?
Girl Oh no! Alex was teaching his sister how to ride a bicycle.
Teacher And....?
Girl And they went down a hill too fast.....he was showing off.....and they both fell off!

Tape 20a

Paul What are you doing?
Sally I'm writing a story.
Lisa Let's see. 'The man walked along the street.'
Sally What do you think?
Lisa Well, it's a little boring. Why not change it to 'The old man walked along the street'?
Paul Yes, or 'The tall, grey-haired old man walked along the street.'
Sally OK. 'The tall, grey-haired old man walked.....'
Paul Hey, wait a minute.....make it more interesting.....'The strange, tall, thin, grey-haired old man walked along the long, dark, quiet street.' How about that?
Lisa Yes, that's better.
Paul OK. What's next?
Sally 'He was wearing a coat and hat.'
Lisa Oh, no! 'He was wearing a long, thick, warm, expensive, black fur coat.....'
Paul '.....and an elegant, new, black and red hat.'
Sally Right. That's much more interesting.
Lisa Well, what comes next?

136

Tape 20b

Girl 1 What do you want to be when you grow up?
Girl 2 I want to be a cook.
Girl 1 A cook? Why?
Girl 2 Because it's an interesting job. And I like food!

Boy 1 What do you want to be?
Boy 2 I want to be a reporter.
Boy 1 Why?
Boy 2 Well . . . . . because it's exciting. Reporters travel to interesting places and meet interesting people.

Boy 3 What do you want to be?
Boy 4 A pop star.
Boy 3 A pop star! Why?
Boy 4 Because I like singing and playing guitar – and I want to be rich!

Boy 5 What do you want to be?
Boy 6 I want to be a doctor.
Boy 5 Why?
Boy 6 It's a good job. Doctors look after people and make them healthy. It's a good thing to do.

Boy 7 I want to be a farmer when I grow up.
Girl 3 Why?
Boy 7 Because I like animals, and I like to be outside in the fresh air.

Girl 4 What do you want to be when you grow up?
Boy 8 A mechanic. I like cars, and I like mending things. It's an interesting job.

Tape 21a

Teacher Who did this exhibition? Peter, was it you?
Peter No, Sir, it was Karim!
Karim No, Sir, it wasn't me! John did it.
Teacher John?
John I didn't do it! I wasn't here!
Teacher So, who was it? Reda?
Reda It wasn't me. Maybe Alex did it.

Alex No, I didn't. It was Walid.
Walid It was not, Sir! Paul and Tom did it.

Paul and Tom We didn't. It wasn't us. It was Adam.
Adam No, it wasn't.

Teacher So . . . . . NOBODY did it . . . . . is that right?
Well, I think EVERYBODY did it. So EVERYBODY must get a prize!

Tape 21b

Peter OK, Karim. Which planet is nearest to the sun?
Karim Mercury.
Peter Yes, that's right. Two points for Team A.

Tom Right, Peter, which is bigger – Mars or Earth?
Peter Mars.
Tom No, it's the Earth.

John Tom, which is the longest river in the world?
Tom The Nile.
John Yes. That's two points for Team A.

Alex John. What is the biggest island in the world?
John Uh . . . . . Australia?
Alex Yes! Two points for Team B.
Reda When did Bill Clinton become President of the USA, Alex?
Alex 1990?
Reda No, it was 1992.

Walid	Paul, when did Gorbachev become Premier of Russia?
Paul	Oh, I don't know . . . . . uh . . . . . 1985?
Walid	Yes . . . . . Two points for Team B.
Paul	Which sport did Pele play?
Walid	That's easy . . . . . football.
Paul	Yes. Two points for Team A.
Karim	Which sport does Boris Becker play, Reda?
Reda	Uh . . . . . golf . . . . . no, tennis!
Karim	OK. Two points for Team B. That's six points each!

Tape 21c

Narrator Every year over 50000 books and half a million newspapers and magazines are made in Braille, the special alphabet for blind people. This alphabet was invented by a Frenchman, Louis Braille.

Louis Braille was born in France in 1809. When he was about three years old, Louis had an accident. He hurt his eye with a knife and, after only six months, Louis was blind.

Louis went to a special school for the blind, in Paris. He began to think about the problem of reading. He decided to make a special alphabet for blind people. Instead of using letters, he wanted to use a kind of code. After many years' work, he thought of the six dots on a domino. With these six dots he could make sixty-three different patterns! He used these patterns for letters and for short, common words like *and, for, with, of, the* and for maths signs.

When books are made for blind people the patterns of dots are pressed onto the page. Blind people 'read' Braille by feeling the raised dots with their fingers.

Louis Braille later worked as a teacher at his old school in Paris. He died in 1852, aged 43. He had helped blind people all over the world, with his six 'magic' dots.

Tape 22a

Interviewer	Good evening, everybody. Well, on tonight's programme we have Terry Mann, the star football player. Good evening, Terry.
Terry	Good evening.
Interviewer	Well, now, Terry, tell me – do you like your job?
Terry	Yes . . . . . very much. I enjoy playing football – I think it's an exciting game. And I like the team, too. Yes – it's a great job.
Interviewer	What do you like best about it?
Terry	Playing together with the other members of the team.
Interviewer	Is there any part of the job you don't like?
Terry	Oh . . . . . getting up early and working out on the field. I hate that, especially in winter!
Interviewer	Now . . . . . How do you relax?
Terry	Oh, I like other sports.
Interviewer	Yes? Which sports do you play?
Terry	Golf, tennis, uh . . . . . swimming, too.
Interviewer	Are sports your only hobby?
Terry	Well, I travel, too . . . . . you know, on holiday.
Interviewer	I see. Who goes with you?
Terry	Oh, my wife and my two sons.
Interviewer	And where do you like to go?
Terry	Switzerland.
Interviewer	Why do you like Switzerland?
Terry	Oh, I like skiing very much. And I like the food in Switzerland, too.
Interviewer	What's your favourite food?
Terry	Uh . . . . . lobster, I think. Yes, lobster.
Interviewer	Well, Terry, the thing everybody wants to know now is . . . . . when are you moving to a new team?
Terry	Oh, I don't think I'm going to move yet. I'm very happy where I am.
Interviewer	Well, good luck in next week's game, and thank you for talking to us.
Terry	Thank you.

Tape 22b

Jane Hello. 645327.
Clare Hello. Is that you, Jane?
Jane Yes. Who's speaking?
Clare It's me . . . . . Clare.
Jane Clare! Hello! Well, what a surprise! How are you?
Clare I'm fine, thanks. I'm just here for a short visit. I'm staying with my cousin, in Green Road.
Jane That's great! Can you come and see us? We'd like to see you again.
Clare Well . . . . . I can't come, really. I'm only here until tomorrow afternoon . . . . . then I'm flying back.
Jane OK, well, never mind. What's your news? You're still living in Canada, then?
Clare Yes . . . . . I love it. I like my job and I like the Canadians. They're very friendly. Actually, I'm getting married next month.
Jane Oh, congratulations! Are you going to marry a Canadian?
Clare Yes.
Jane What's he like?
Clare Oh, he's very nice! He's a doctor.
Jane How did you meet him?
Clare Oh, we met at the hospital when I broke my leg.
Jane How did you break your leg?
Clare Well . . . . . I go skiing every weekend – but I'm not very good so I often have accidents like that!
Jane Well, it's so nice to talk to you. I'm glad you're happy. Perhaps we can come to Canada and visit you soon.
Clare Yes . . . . . that's a good idea!

Tape 22c

Exercise A

1	please,	police	**6**	this,	this
2	price,	prize	**7**	close (adj),	close (v)
3	race,	raise	**8**	as,	as
4	size,	size	**9**	cross,	cross
5	use (v),	use (n)	**10**	eyes,	ice

Exercise B

1	air,	hair	**6**	hate,	eight
2	had,	add	**7**	ear,	hear
3	hand,	and	**8**	eat,	heat
4	as,	has	**9**	hill,	ill
5	at,	hat	**10**	his,	is

Tape 23a

Boy 1 What are you doing on Friday?
Girl 1 I'm having a barbecue. Would you like to come?
Boy 1 Yes, please.
Girl 1 Bring an umbrella.
Boy 1 An umbrella? Why?
Girl 1 Well, it might rain.

Boy 2 What are you doing tomorrow?
Girl 2 I'm going to the cinema. I'm seeing the new Indiana Jones film. Are you coming?
Boy 2 No, thanks. My grandmother might come tomorrow.

Boy 3 What are you doing for your holiday?
Girl 3 I'm going to Malaysia with my family. Are you going away?
Boy 3 I'm not sure. We might go to Turkey . . . . . but I don't know yet.

Tape 23b

Girl Do you want to play football with me?
Boy No.
Girl Are you working?
Boy No.
Girl Are you reading?
Boy Yes.

Girl	What are you reading?
Boy	A book!
Girl	Why are you reading it?
Boy	Because it's very exciting.
Girl	When are you going to finish it?
Boy	I don't know! Sssh!
Girl	Can I borrow it?
Boy	No. It's not my book.
Girl	Whose is it then?
Boy	It's Paul's. Now be quiet!
Girl	Which Paul? Paul Smith?
Boy	No, Paul Green.
Girl	Is it interesting?
Boy	Yes.
Girl	What is it about?
Boy	It's a spy story.
Girl	Who is the spy?
Boy	I don't know yet. Now be quiet and let me read!

Tape 23c

Mrs Field	Oh, this weekend was terrible!
Friend	Why? What happened?
Mrs Field	Well . . . . . on Saturday night I was having a bath and washing my hair. My husband was painting the kitchen ceiling. John was watching TV with two of his friends. Penny was making some trousers.
Friend	That's not so terrible, is it?
Mrs Field	Well . . . . . at 7 o'clock Mr and Mrs Booth arrived! We invited them for dinner last week, but I forgot all about it!
Friend	Oh, no!

Tape 24a

1 ear   **2** bed   **3** vote   **4** prize   **5** hat

Tape 24b

1 and   **2** ice   **3** hair   **4** feet   **5** bet

Tape 25a

Oh, we can play on the big bass drum,
And this is the way we do it.
Boom, boom, boom goes the big bass drum,
And that's the way we do it.

Oh, we can play on the triangle,
And this is the way we do it.
Ting, ting, ting goes the triangle,
And that's the way we do it.

Oh, we can play on the violin,
And this is the way we do it.
Eee, eee, eee goes the violin,
And that's the way we do it.

Oh, we can play on the piano,
And this is the way we do it.
Plink, plink, plonk goes the piano,
And that's the way we do it.

Oh, we can play on the silver flute,
And this is the way we do it.
Toot, toot, toot goes the silver flute,
And that's the way we do it.

Tape 25b

1 cheap,	sheep	**6** washing,	watching
2 change,	change	**7** chops,	shops
3 March,	March	**8** catch,	catch
4 ships,	chips	**9** chew,	shoe
5 shine,	shine	**10** mushroom,	much room